Math for Mystics

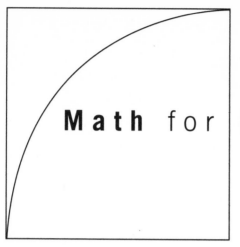

Math for Mystics

From the Fibonacci Sequence
to Luna's Labyrinth
to the Golden Section
and Other Secrets of Sacred Geometry

Renna Shesso

WEISERBOOKS
San Francisco, CA / Newburyport, MA

First published in 2007
by Red Wheel/Weiser, LLC
With offices at:
500 Third Street, Suite 230
San Francisco, CA 94107
www.redwheelweiser.com

ISBN-10: 1-57863-383-4
ISBN-13: 978-1-57863-383-8

Library of Congress Cataloging-in-Publication Data
Shesso, Renna. From the Fibonacci Sequence to Luna's Labyrinth to
the Golden Section and other Secrets of Sacred Geometry/Renna Shesso.
        p. cm.
Includes bibliographical references and index.
 ISBN 1-57863-383-4 (alk. paper)
1. Geometry—Miscellanea. 2. Mathematics—Miscellanea. I. Title.
QA447.S36 2007
516—dc22
2006032047

Cover and interior design by Maija Tollefson
Typeset in Trade Gothic and Grajon
Interior illustrations © 2007 by Renna Shesso
Cover photo illustration © 2007 by Kevin Irby

Printed in Canada
TCP
10 9 8 7 6 5 4 3 2 1

Contents

Introduction: "Math?! Why?"

As human beings, we aren't just mildly curious. We're demandingly curious. We want to understand! We want to know! We want to find the underlying order in our universe! We want to matter! We want to count!

Eek! Count?! No! That sounds like math! How ironic that today, in the twenty-first century-despite technology designed to help us do everything imaginable involving numbers-so many of us are profoundly math-phobic. Friends exchange personal horror stories of grade school math experiences, memories similar to my own, sometimes worse. Enjoy arithmetic? Heck, with the sense of mental abuse some of us absorbed with our multiplication tables, it's a wonder we can even count.

It's our collective malaise: Post-Traumatic Math Disorder.

Yet despite how we personally feel about mathematics, our distant ancestors willingly used numbers as pathways into the great patterns of Nature, avenues to understanding the Universe and their own place in it. Many ancient cultures had specific gods and goddesses they credited with inventing mathematical skills. With the aid of divine inspiration and assistance, humans nourished this numerical invention, continually pushing their skills and seeking greater clarity of expression.

Often, their motivation was metaphysical: A large portion of math history traces back directly to the earliest astrologers, who needed to be able to describe and record what they saw in the night sky. Notably, in math history books, those original innovators are usually referred to as *astronomers*, not astrologers, as if they were either one or the other. Astrology, astronomy . . . initially, the metaphysical and practical worlds overlapped, and it was all the same thing. Whether you were the queen's astrologer or a farmer marking the solstice, timekeeping mattered, and numbers mattered. Mistake a numerical pattern of petals or leaves and you could accidentally poison yourself. Lose the rhythm of a sacred dance, fumble the meter of a ritually told creation story, and the clear patterns of life might be spoiled. Ignore the celestial clock of equinoxes and solstices, and you'd risk being caught short of food as winter arrived. Lose your navigational position at sea . . . well, no good at all.

Striving to understand the order and intelligence they sensed in their surroundings-our surroundings, Mother Earth-our ancestors sought an appropriate language to express what they were learning. The tones and tempos in music, the cadences in speech, the harmonious patterns in weaving or in painted decoration, the embodiment of meaning into architecture, the elegant dance of the stars and planets. . . . These studies overlapped into the realm of the spirit while still requiring a grasp of space, form and dimension, all of which could be expressed numerically. The numbers we know are one means of doing this, but there are other infinitely creative methods. The Mayans used complex mask-like glyphs to record their extremely accurate calendars. Pacific Islanders navigated the open sea guided by chants that mimicked the unique rhythm of waves between islands.

What you'll find in this book are some of the many things our distant ancestors knew and used, based on long generations of seeing and absorbing, based on sky watching, on folk knowledge, on myths and on ever-more-complex calculations. Much of this information quietly feeds the rich foundation for modern-day Wiccan practices. Studying it, I feel as if I'm holding a fistful of very fine and very long threads that I can slowly trace back to their sources. Some of the threads unravel in the process. Some change color or texture and become unrecognizable. Others are still hopelessly tangled. But some threads-those I've included in this book-run true, stay bright, sing when I pluck them, and can still bear the weight of practical use. This certainly isn't all-inclusive, but makes for a reasonable starting point. There are many more strands still waiting to be discovered, untangled, and utilized.

Using This Book

A surprising number of vintage numerology books start out speaking in spiritual terms but ultimately shift to picking horses at the race track, Let's capriciously assume that gambling is not a major concern here. When I look at numbers in a metaphysical context, I'm usually getting ready to do spellwork, the magical action of graphically sending forth my intentions and requests to the Celestial Powers-That-Be. Do I want to use four different herbs in my talisman? Would five herbs be better? How many knots should I tie to close the pouch? Why? Does the choice of day matter? How come? We'll explore this type of number-question in the following pages.

Despite the dreaded M-word in the title (and I don't mean Mystics), there's very little actual math required here. One concept that is necessary is knowing how to reduce multidigit numbers. Since this generally isn't covered in "real" math classes, I'll explain it here. For many magical and numerology purposes, we add together the digits of multidigit numbers to produce simpler numbers, those from 1 to 9. Sadly, this has no practical application like calculating sales tax or balancing a checkbook.

It's just a simple principle that appears frequently in metaphysical number use.

So, when the text advises you to "reduce" a number, that's all it means: Add the multiple digits together as if each digit were an independent number. When you need to end up with a single digit, keep going until you get there. For example 15, the number of the Devil card in the Tarot deck, when reduced becomes 6 (from 1 + 5), the same number as the Lovers card, which certainly provides food for thought.

Dates are handled a little differently, as demonstrated in *Figure I-1*:

A.   12   *B.* 1   *C.* 2   **Figure I-1 Adding**
    31   9   +2   A. December 31, 1950 is reduced as
+1950   9   4   12 (month) + 31 (day) + 1950 (year) = 1993
 1993   +3   B. Then 1 + 9 + 9 + 3 = 22
           22   C. Followed by 2 + 2 = 4

This is basic pencil-and-paper stuff, so don't bother buying batteries for the calculator.

A Math (and Art) Fable

As a child, Pablo Picasso could draw brilliantly, but was hopeless in mathematics. He supposedly explained that he got distracted by how the numbers looked. To the young Pablo, the number-glyph that meant 2 just looked like a swan. The glyph meaning 5 seemed more like an eyebrow jutting over a large nose. The numbers were distracting him from math: Rather than seeing them as symbols, Picasso saw the numbers as nonquantifiable shapes.

Figure I-2 Picasso 2   **Figure I-3** Picasso 5

Whether or not it's true, this story remains popular among art students.

"I became an artist because they promised there wouldn't be any math."
—From an artist friend

The Circle of Creation

A cat in a vintage cartoon plucks a Zero off a sign and tosses the symbol against a wall. The Zero transforms into a round hole, a portal, and the cat leaps through.

Our starting point may seem like a Zero. But for now, before looking at numbers and math, let's simply see it as a circle. No matter what our spiritual practice, we each live within the circle of creation, each within the circle—the cohesiveness—of our own form.

This is an opening consideration about human form and how we use it. We may feel comfortable with it. Or not. In a sense, what we do with our lives, how much joy and satisfaction we experience, will be based on how well we get along with "the equipment," the form we inhabit and the spirit that infuses it.

This book takes its themes from our shared human history, our ancestral means of attempting to understand the human condition and the world around us. The long mixture of people from whom we're descended had plenty of questions about the Earth and the Universe and their place in it all. One of the ways they explored these questions was through numbers.

Numbers exist throughout nature—petals on a flower, stars in a constellation, fingers and toes, and the phases of the Moon. Quantity. Time. Rhythm. Math is our way of exploring and expressing this aspect of Nature. Math can't convey the scent of a flowering apple tree, but we can count five petals on each blossom. Later, we see a five-lobed star of seeds when we cut the fruit in half horizontally. Traditional metaphysical correspondences associate the apple with the planet Venus. Why? If we trace back farther, we'll find what many early people knew: Venus draws a pentacle in its orbit. The apple and the pentacle gradually came to be associated with the goddess of love. There are mathematical means of tracking Venus' orbit and her tenure as Evening Star versus Morning Star, but unless the scent of the apple blossom can be part of our equation, too, we risk missing the point.

Aroma communicates vividly, dodging past logic, and zooming directly to the senses. And the senses take us back to the question of the human form and the human experience. We're capable of understanding so much with our fabulous minds! We can be so enamored and brainwashed by logic that we forget: We can also connect with reality through the senses and the heart.

American culture is not one that's comfortable with senses, heart, or intuitive ways of knowing. Most of us have been admonished since childhood to "Use your head!" and "Think!" The phrase "What were you thinking?!" may have come in the same breath as "Don't let your imagination run away with you."

Intuition sparked our little-kid panic when we heard our parents arguing with each other. Whether or not we understood their words, we could feel their tension. Our intuitive response to their anger was "My security is at risk!" But our intuition probably got shot down if we expressed our fears: "No, honey, Mommy and Daddy aren't mad at each other. Nothing's wrong." Maybe no one was lying, exactly—their argument was indeed trivial, and no danger or loss would follow—but in reassuring us of our safety in this way, the well-intentioned parent implicitly told us that we couldn't trust our intuition.

If this happened only once during childhood, it wouldn't have much impact. But for many of us, versions of this scenario happened repeatedly. Our intuition—a crucial human survival tool, eons in the making and closely wired in to the senses—was denounced and at least partially dismantled. Our instinct about what and whom we can trust—*starting with ourselves*—was branded untrustworthy. Logic became king.

And logic loves numbers. Somewhere along the line, our ability to count, to quantify, got perverted into the mistaken idea that everything is or should be quantifiable. There's no room here for the evocative aroma of the blossom-laden apple tree gleaming white in the moonlight, but the supposed trade-off is gigantic: Logic will keep us safe, fear-and anxiety-free, stable and sane.

Except, of course, it can't. Changes occur, and we need all of our resources—including intuition and imagination and instinct—to adapt, survive, and flourish.

We know inherently how much we need our intuitive senses, so is it any surprise if we gradually become distrustful of logic? This logic backlash happens especially when we start to explore spiritual paths, avenues that encourage the senses and intuition. Some numerology systems reflect this discomfort: They give us numbers, sure, but real math is allowed in only begrudgingly and in the most simplistic terms.

Unfortunately, that's the practical equivalent of seeing Thor's hammer, Mjollnir, as just a symbol rather than as a practical tool. Hey, that thing's fine as a tattoo or necklace charm, but wow, don't actually hit anything!

In mythology, Thor *uses* his hammer, creating thunder and lightning, forging alliances, shaking things up and opening the way for change, whether the changes arrive through chaos and upheaval, through flashes of insight and comprehension, or through the slow, steady glow of enlightenment.

That's what tools do. They help us effect intentional change.

And, at their best, numbers are tools.

That's why we're starting at Zero. This circle, this Zero, can be a doorway, a portal. Just as Zero serves as a placeholder in math, it becomes the placeholding circle I create when I call the quarters, marking off space "between the worlds," inviting in those energies that will serve my purpose, while keeping other energies at bay.

Zero can be an excellent circle of protection if—like me—you grew up being cautioned about the dangers of an "overactive imagination." Imaginary friends? Conversations with deceased grandparents? A simple sense of the numinous in Nature? As young humans using all the senses we were born with, we hadn't learned yet to ignore those that made other people profoundly nervous. Instead of our inborn awareness being nourished and encouraged, we were directed instead toward fact and logic: "Use your head!"

Logic isn't the problem: Divorcing it from heart and spirit is. Being told to "Think!" often meant "Don't feel!" How significant that a common image of "magic" is a stage magician sawing a woman in half. Modern culture fractures our awareness, women and men alike, encouraging our fragmentation into jigsaw puzzles of varying roles, mistrustful of our senses and of logic, and too often at odds with various aspects of ourselves.

In that place of vulnerability, we *need* a circle of protection. Within it, we can move toward retraining our sense of intuition gradually and gently. One way to do that, as a bridge between two supposedly opposite ways of knowing, is to reapproach numbers and math like we're meeting them for the first time, letting imagination run away as much as it likes, to a place where intuition and logic become allies. The real act of magic is the reassembly of self.

And here Zero is again, not as "nothing," but as a circle, a symbol of wholeness and continuity. Like an empty vessel, it stands wide open, ready to "hold the space" for us, inviting us in where all is possible.

Onward through the portal. . . .

CHAPTER 1

Counting

"He counts using his fingers." Nowadays, that phrase is generally an unkind one, a snippy way of implying that a person isn't very bright. Once upon a time, though, counting on our fingers had sacred connotations, and to know the number of things was itself an act of magic. Our word *ritual* comes from the Indo-European root *ri*, which means "to count, to number."[1] The association of *ri* with "ritual" comes from the use of rites to mark the seasons of the year, back in the days when a comprehension of time and seasons could be crucial to survival. Clearly, our personal ancestors succeeded in their season-counting and winter food storage, or we wouldn't be here now. We can take that to mean that we all have some inherent aptitude for timekeeping and calculating. In other words, we each have an aptitude for practical math.

Even before the advent of written numbers, people had ways of enumerating quantities. We could cut or scratch notches on a spare piece of bone (many examples of this have survived) or we could line up stones (which would then get scattered), or we could use our fingers. The Sanskrit word for "finger-counting" is *mûdrâ*, closely related to *mudrâ*, the word for the symbolic hand gestures seen in Hindu religious statuary and sacred dance.[2] Maybe you do your own little finger dances while you drive, drumming out basslines in time with the radio, as rhythm divides time. Without consciously saying, "One, two, three, and four . . . ," you're counting, in the most primal way, as body-knowledge. Forget multiplication tables! Give me a turntable!

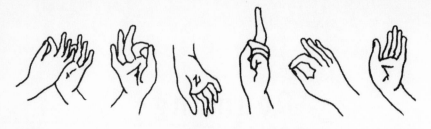

Figure 1-1 There are many *mudrâ* gestures. Left to right, these six are *Dharmachakra* ("teachings of law"), *Vitarka* ("argument"), *Varada* ("conferring grace"), *Tarjani* ("warning"), *Jnana* ("teaching"), and *Abhaya* ("protection").

It's hard to imagine looking at our ten dancing fingers and not evolving a system based on 10. Those ten fingers—I mean, really, what else could we have done? Ah, but people using the same standard-issue hands did come up with other options. Read on.

Zero and Nine

In 773 CE, a diplomatic mission from northern India arrived in Baghdad.[3] From Baghdad to northern India is roughly 1,500 miles, minimum. As modern humans, we tend to forget our most primal Road Trip roots. Chances are we had distant ancestors who spent not hours, but days, weeks, months—or years—physically getting to a location that really mattered to them. The Indian delegation made what must have been an unimaginably arduous journey.

This visiting Indian contingent included an astronomer/astrologer named Kanaka. Though the studies of astronomy and astrology are now firmly separated, they originally evolved together, and the Indians were considered especially skilled. Caliph al-Mansur, the Arabian host, became so impressed with Kanaka's star skills that he had Arabic translations made of the Indian reference works Kanaka had brought along. These translations were avidly shared, copied and recopied (by hand, of course), studied, discussed and mentally digested among Arabian astrologers, and about 50 years later, an original work by Arab mathematician al-Khuwarizmi appeared. Called *Kitab al jam' wa'l tafriq bi hisab al hind* ("Indian technique of addition and subtraction"), al-Khuwarizmi's text concerned the still-novel Indian numbers that had so impressed Caliph al-Mansur.[4] Al-Khuwarizmi gave a detailed explanation of decimal numeration, the nine Indian number symbols and "the tenth figure in the shape of a circle" that was used "so as not to confuse the positions" of the numbers.[5]

That "tenth figure in the shape of a circle" was Zero. One theory of its origin: People counted using pebbles laid in rows on a sandy surface. The Indians' term for "higher computations" was *dhuli-kharma*, which actually means "sand-work." Let's put pebbles in rows to represent quantities. To subtract, we remove pebbles. What's left? Some pebbles, of course, as well as faint depressions in the sand. We check our math by looking at the dents left behind by the pebbles we removed. And the shape of each depression would be a soft-edged circle in the sand, now containing nothing.[6]

But let's get back to ancient Arabia. The al-Khuwarizmi text became popular in the Arab world and quietly arrived in Europe during the long Moorish presence in Spain. Although the text seems not to have spread into the rest of Europe, its ideas spread readily in other lands, and by the early eleventh century the Indian numerals and the zero were in common use from the borders of central Asia into northern Africa and Egypt. Undoubtedly, variations on this numerical information migrated not just through Indian astrologers, but through other pragmatic folks as well, since what worked for scholars and astrologers would also be useful to merchants and accountants— to anyone making practical use of numbers. Finally, an abridged copy of al-Khuwarizmi's work, now simply called *Arithmetic*, was translated into Latin in 1126 CE, at which point it quickly became influential and controversial throughout Europe.

Why did *Arithmetic* make such an impact? Because it presented some things Europe didn't have: a consistent and simple way to write the numbers 1 though 9, and the radically innovative placeholder, zero. What we came to call the "Arabic numerals"—since they reached Europe through translations from the Arabic—in fact have their roots deeply in India. The legendary brilliance of Indian astronomer-astrologers like Kanaka was credited to their superior skill in mathematics, skills made easier by their numerical system. Cuneiform and Roman numerals are okay for writing, and pebbles or fingers work fine for counting, but neither is math-friendly. Astrologers needed writeable math formulae capable of greater complexity, and by creatively pushing to discover better and more detailed ways to express numbers, the ancient Indians moved to the forefront in astrology, astronomy, and math.

Not everyone approved of the new-style written numbers. "Quantities" weren't—and aren't—the same as "numbers." The former are visible objects, like sheep or apples, while the latter, those "numbers," are nothing more than weird shapes scrawled on a page. Zeros are especially suspect: Pen a tail on 0 and it becomes 6 or 9. Tag on extra zeros, and that bogus 9 becomes 90, 900, 9,000, or worse. Small wonder that eleventh-century monk-historian William of Malmesbury considered the newfangled Indian-Arabic numerals, and especially that pesky zero, to be "dangerous Saracen magic."[7]

Back to trustworthy finger-counting. For the record, you can count to 9 on one hand using your five fingers and the spaces between them. The odd numbers land on the fingers, and the gaps get the even numbers—5 odd, 4 even—and it works perfectly. The Chinese believed that even numbers were bad luck and odd numbers were lucky. Perhaps this stemmed from even numbers landing on between-fingers nothingness. The Pythagoreans simply believed that even numbers were female and odd numbers were male, without the more pejorative good-or-bad-luck connotation.[8] That gender distinction could have been based on how these numbers are counted on the human hand: The "male" odd numbers land

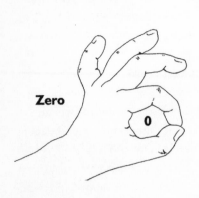

Figure 1-2 Zero

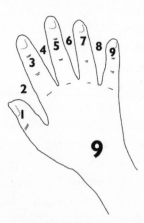

Figure 1-3 Hand counting 9

on the projecting fingers, and the "female" even numbers nestle in the open crevices between fingers. Pretty graphic, pretty basic.

Nines have their own category of math tricks. For instance, any number multiplied by 9 "reduces" to 9. Try this with 18, 27, 36, 45, and any other multiplied-by-9 sum, and in each case you'll get 9, a good memory trick for 9's multiplication table. When written together, those multiplied-by-9 sums create a numerical *palindrome*—9, 18, 27, 36, 45, 54, 63, 72, 81, 99—which (except for the doubled 99) reads the same backward and forward.

There's another old trick, dating back to at least the tenth century, called "casting out nines."[9] Flip back to the "Using This Book" section in the Introduction and look at the total for December 31, 1950: 1993. Reduced, the sum was 4. That's the same sum we can get immediately from 1993 by just adding 1 + 3 and "casting out"—that is, ignoring—the two 9s, which will cancel themselves out in the next step anyway. Nines void themselves out—at least they have every time I've tested this. Why does this work? I understand it—sort of—but happily it works whether or not I can explain it to myself.

Twelve

Look at one of your hands. The index finger is also called the "pointer," and point it does, at least when we're looking at something beyond that hand. But when we're counting on a single hand, the thumb is generally the built-in pointer. It's an easy and automatic gesture, useful when enumerating small amounts, but only small amounts.

Or maybe not. Each of the four fingers has three easily seen joints. Our pointer-thumbs can reach each finger joint and count to 12 using them. Did the Babylonians, who had a 60-based number system, use one hand's twelve finger joints to count to 12 and use the other hand's five fingers for tracking how many times they'd done so—12, 24, 36, 48, 60?

We still buy eggs by twelves, and other things, too, like fresh cookies and flowers. We have 12 months and 12 astrological signs, and 12 inches in a foot, so the number has some practical applications. Some sources credit the word *dozen* as coming from the Latin for "two" and "ten"—*duo-decem*—shortened

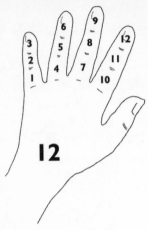

Figure 1-4 Hand counting 12

gradually to dozen. Others trace it back to an ancient Sumerian word that meant "a fifth of sixty."[10] Twelve is wonderfully useful. It can be evenly divided by 2, 3, 4, and 6, and its multiples include significant numbers like 24 (hours in a day), 60 (number systems, seconds, minutes), 108 (the Buddhist *mala* or prayer beads), 144 (a gross), and 360 (the number of degrees in a circle). We'll look at circles more closely later.

Fourteen

Now let's go a step—two steps—further. If we include the thumb in our joint-counting, our number becomes 14. Unlike the fingers, the thumb has only two readily visible joints. While 14 isn't a number that readily springs to mind like "dozen," it's had its uses. A fortnight is 2 weeks, literally 14 nights, shortened from *fourteen-night*. In pre-metric Britain, if you said something weighed "a stone," you meant 14 pounds. The ancient Chinese, Assyrians, Babylonians, and Sumerians all counted to 14 on the finger-and-thumb joints.

The number 14 doesn't do as many tricks as 9 or crop up as often as 12, but it has a longtime magical correlation that would have made it important to many ancient people: the Moon. See Chapter 2 for a look at this connection.

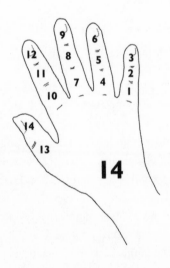

Figure 1-5 Hand counting 14

Fifteen and More

Other handy hand-counts of yore include an Indian and Bengali count of 15 (the 14-count plus the pad at the base of the thumb) to track their 15-day "months," each half a lunar cycle in length. Twenty-four of these made up their 360-day year. A Muslim version of 15 used both hands to count to 30, then added the tips of three fingers to reach 33, repeated thrice when reciting the 99 attributes of Allah.[11]

The Venerable Bede (673–735 CE, a monk who wrote *De ratione temporum—Of the Division of Time*) tracked an important lunar cycle by counting 19 years on finger joints and tips, thumb joints and thumb pad of the left hand.[12] Called the "Metonic cycle" (for Meton, a fifth-century BCE Athenian astronomer), this tracks the Moon's motions as they repeat every 19 years, with Earth's natural satellite in the same phase, sign, degree, and declination on the same day of the month.[13]

For a dramatic example, here are Full Moon eclipses in 1991 and 2010:[14]
1991, December 21: Moon at 29° Gemini, 24° N declination
2010, December 21: Moon at 29° Gemini, 24° N declination

Dice: The Fickle Finger of Fate?

Gambling with dice or "knuckles bones" has some loose but logical ties back to finger-counting.[15] The earliest dice were real knuckle bones, roughly cubical bones from the toes of various critters. Called *astragali* (a reference to Astraea, goddess of justice), they were used for games of chance, but also came into play for making legal decisions, such as dividing inheritances or sharing out temple income, even for selecting government officials. In the geometric "Platonic" solids, the cube symbolizes Earth. That's fitting, since in some ancient cases, the cube-shaped dice influenced earthly, practical matters.

The Assyrians were the first to make clay dice, more evenly shaped than the irregular bones. In northern Europe, the invention of dice was credited to clever Woden, deity of wisdom and prophecy. Our words *lot* (as in parcel of land), *lottery*, and *allotment* all have their roots in the throwing of lots with dice. To say you "cast your lot" with someone meant you were gambling your own fortune and luck with theirs.

The words—singular *die*, plural *dice*—come from the Low Latin *dadus*, meaning "given," as in "given by the gods."[16] Luck at dice wasn't viewed as pure random chance: Winning was a cosmic sign that the gods were smiling upon you.

These pagan associations were a perfect setup for the church to condemn dice as yet another of the devil's innumerable playthings. Besides, why leave temple profits, inheritances, and government jobs to the dicey whims of pagan deities?

Incidentally, dice needn't be six-sided cubes. Eight-sided octahedron dice have been discovered in Egyptian tombs (interesting: an octahedron is the shape of two pyramids joined at their bases), while dodecahedron (twelve-sided) and icosahedron (twenty-sided) dice were sometimes used by early fortune-tellers. Perhaps this was due to their respective Platonic associations with ethereal Spirit and emotional Water, or maybe it was simply the fortune-tellers' bid for more repeat business, by having even more possible answers available.

There are twenty-one possible combinations when rolling a pair of cubical dice:

1-1, 1-2, 1-3, 1-4, 1-5, 1-6
2-2, 2-3, 2-4, 2-5, 2-6
3-3, 3-4, 3-5, 3-6
4-4, 4-5, 4-6
5-5, 5-6
6-6

Add up all the dots on a single die—1 + 2 + 3 + 4 + 5 + 6—and the total is 21.

CHAPTER 2

The Moon

How many neopagans does it take to tell what phase the Moon is in? A surprising number of us depend on printed calendars rather than our own eyes to tell us if the Moon is waxing or waning. Tsk, tsk! This primal piece of cosmic timekeeping can help us easily tap into a deeper cyclical awareness of time.

Some of this happens at a physiological level, in our own bodies. Young women are often told at puberty that a "normal" menstrual cycle is 28 days long. What is seldom mentioned (at least in mundane environs) is that the Moon and the menstrual cycle can move together. Like the tides of the ocean, drawn higher by the Moon's gravitational pull, the small ocean of the human body responds to the Moon, too. Women are said to be more likely to begin labor around the Full Moon, and once upon a time, women may have ovulated near the Full Moon and bled near the New Moon.

The menstrual cycle is still called the "moon time," but according to some theories, women in industrialized nations have been knocked out of harmony with the lunar cycle by all the artificial lights that illuminate the modern night. Few of us now sleep in such total darkness that the cyclical waxing and waning light of the Moon is noticeable to the responsive physiology of the light-sensitive pineal gland in our "third eye" area. There may be ways of getting back in sync (first, sleep in total darkness; then, use a night light on the 3 nights when the Moon is fullest[1]), but one tiny miscalculation remains in these proceedings:

The Moon's cycle isn't really 28 days. *(See Figure 2-1.)* From New Moon to New Moon, the Moon's cycle in relation to the Sun is between 29 and 30 days. This is called the *synodic* month, and its precise average is 29 days, 12 hours, 44 minutes and 3 seconds—29.53 days. Our earliest ancestors were already tracking it roughly 30,000–35,000 years ago, making clusters of scratch-marks on bones, antlers, and cavern walls, sometimes showing 29 scratches, sometimes 30.[2,3]

Meanwhile, Luna's monthly journey through the twelve constellations of the zodiac is on a slightly different schedule. Based on the relation to the stars rather than to the Sun, and called the *sidereal* month, the Moon's star-oriented circuit averages 27 days, 7 hours, 43 minutes, and 12 seconds. If the synodic and sidereal months were exactly synchronized, the Full Moon would be in the same sign of the zodiac every month. But it isn't (and how boring if it were).

Instead, just as the Sun progresses one zodiac sign per month, so does the Full Moon. Full Moons happen when the Sun and Moon are opposite each other in our sky, so whatever sign the Sun is in, the Full Moon will be—*must* be—in the opposite sign of the zodiac. Since it's based on the backdrop of stars behind the Moon, this Moon cycle isn't nearly as obvious as her cycle of shape-changing phases.

So where did the association of the Moon with the number 28 come from? The New Moon—shown as a solid black circle on calendars—occurs when the Moon and Sun are conjunct, aligned with each other in the same astrological sign as seen from Earth. Except, of course, the Moon *isn't* seen at

Think about it:
If the Moon's cycle was really 28 days, we'd mark the phases every 7th day. Our calendar would look more like this—

S	M	T	W	T	F	S
●						
◑						
○						
◐						
●						
◑						
○						
◐						

—and I bet the day they all landed on would be called Mo(o)nday. But Luna ignores our 7-day week.

Figure 2-1 Moon-weeks

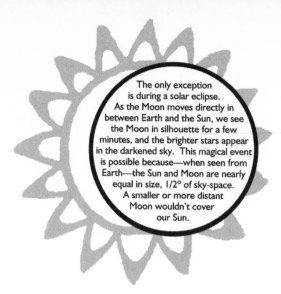

The only exception is during a solar eclipse. As the Moon moves directly in between Earth and the Sun, we see the Moon in silhouette for a few minutes, and the brighter stars appear in the darkened sky. This magical event is possible because—when seen from Earth—the Sun and Moon are nearly equal in size, 1/2° of sky-space. A smaller or more distant Moon wouldn't cover our Sun.

Figure 2-2 Solar eclipse and text

that time. *(See Figure 2-2.)* It's in between the Earth and the Sun, so we'd have to look directly into the Sun to find the Moon at all. Even then, the Moon's lit "face" is facing the Sun while the shadowed side faces us. We can't see it.

So those persistent 28 days can be the days when the Moon might actually be visible, not black-circle-on-the-calendar "new" and conjunct the Sun. Why count what we can't see? We first see the Moon when it moves out of conjunction as a barely visible crescent, poetically called "Diana's Bow," in the western sunset sky. That's when it's visibly "new" to us, beginning its latest cycle. Under optimum conditions—open terrain, clear sky, sharp eye—we might spot the tiniest crescent one day after the calendar's New Moon. Usually it's at least another day before it's visible, weather and terrain permitting.

Thrice-Greatest Hermes

Few deities have numbers clearly incorporated into their names. Though sometimes written of as an historical mathematician, Hermes Trismegistus—Thrice-Great Hermes—is the Egyptian god Aah-Tehuti, or Thoth. Among his innumerable titles and tasks, he was the measurer and regulator in charge of time and season; he was the heart and tongue of the supreme god Ra; he was the teacher of all ancient wisdom; he was Logos, the Creative Word.

The name *Tehuti* may have come from *tehu*, an early Egyptian word meaning "ibis," a bird with a very thin, very curved beak, reminiscent of the slender Crescent Moon. But Tehuti's name may also trace back to *tekh*, a word related to both "weight" and "heart."[4] This is very apropos, since Tehuti supervised the ceremony of weighing the heart of the deceased, balancing the person's heart against Truth, personified by the goddess Ma'at. In depictions of this ceremony, Ma'at was often symbolized by her token, a feather, since truth is weightless, as a true heart would be. Ibis-headed Tehuti/Thoth stood nearby, recording the results, "weighing the words," here taken to mean not spoken language but the inmost expressions of the soul itself.[5]

In addition to his portrayal as a man with the head of an ibis, Thoth was also depicted as the dog-headed ape. When the apes barked at the rising Sun, they were announcing the day and marking time. The ibis and ape were each thought to be the wisest of their kind, bird and mammal, and only the wisest could symbolize Thoth.

In his role as celestial timekeeper, Thoth was associated with the Moon. A mural on the wall of the great temple at Dendera shows Thoth as "Lord of the Moon," enthroned at the top of a staircase. Fourteen steps lead up to him, like the nights leading from the dark of the Moon to Full—Thoth sits on the top, fifteenth step—and the same fourteen steps lead back down as the Moon wanes away.[6] But Thoth wasn't himself the Moon god—rather he was the god who understood and tracked the Moon's motion.

This was a vital task for the Egyptians, since the Moon's symbolism carried into so much of their culture. For instance, the Nile River rose each year, inundating the land and revivifying the soil. A "good inundation" was crucial to agriculture. Measured at Elephantine, the inundation ideally reached 28 cubits in depth, a number related to the full lunar cycle. At Memphis, the maximum depth would be 14 cubits, equated with the Full Moon.[7] As Lord of Rebirth, Thoth helped order and record this.

Thoth's cult-city was Khemennu (or Khmûn, later called Hermopolis), which meant "City of Eight Gods," or the eighth city along the Upper Nile. And the number 8 leads us back to Thoth/Hermes' title of "Thrice-Greatest." An ancient prayer says, "I am One who becomes Two; I am Two who becomes Four; I am Four who becomes Eight; I am the One after that": three mathematical steps of transformation.[8] The other eight gods were seen as contrasting pairs of deities, male/female, positive/negative, active/passive, just the kind of light/dark duality we might expect to see in a Moon-related deity.[9] Eight—or three steps to reach 8 by math—is a recurring number for Tehuti, who in some prayers is addressed as "Thoth, the Eight-times-great, the Lord of Khmûn, the Great God."[10]

Elsewhere in the extensive Hermes Trismegistus literature—often composed in the form of teaching by Thrice-Greatest Hermes for his son Tat (another spelling of Thoth)—we find more numbers. In one missive we find an unhappy Twelve, here being twelve "Torments of Darkness"—although only those living in error will be tormented—while Ten is presented as the number "which gives birth to souls."

Twelve is described here as the "Going-Forth." Associated with the twelve signs of the zodiac, it might be seen as the timed-based journey of human existence, as we strive to understand the Earth-life. This knowledge-seeking phase is portrayed as multiplication-based—that is, 3 x 4, 2 x 6—just as "multiplying" ourselves is a concern of human existence.

Ten is described as "The Return." Representing a resolution of the life quest, it is reached more simply through addition, that is, 7 + 3. The list of Ten positive attributes is Gnosis, Joy, Self-Control, Continence, Righteousness, Sharing-with-All, Truth, The Good, Life and Light.[11]

Although the words *Hermes* and *hermit* have different roots, the figure on the Tarot's Hermit card, number 9 in the Major Arcana, is often shown carrying a lantern. Unlike a candle, a lantern encloses its light, making the Hermit's symbol one of enlightenment.

Although geographically and culturally we're accustomed to things going left to right—how we read, for example, how our clock hands rotate, and the stars and planets moving east to west, left to right, across the sky—Moon *phases* are tracked from right to left as we face south. Sitting in a circle, pass an object to the person on your left—it will return eventually from your right, having traveled clockwise, also called *sunwise* or *deosil*. If you pass the object to your right, it will come back around to your left hand, having gone counter-clockwise, also called *moon-wise* or *widdershins*. It never made sense to me that counter-clockwise was literally "moon-wise" until I learned to track the Moon as if passing it to my right, going "around the circle" of the zodiac to return to my left hand.

When we first see the new Crescent Moon low in the western sky just after sunset, its super-slim shape is like a backward-*C* made by the right hand. *(See Figure 2-3.)* Even though its "horns" point up like a shallow dish, that tilted dish will best fit your right hand. We might say, "It looks like a fingernail clipping." Begin counting on the joints of the right hand's little finger. Watch each evening at sunset, and the Moon will be a little higher in the western sky, farther behind and farther to the left of the Sun. The Moon will be a little wider each evening as well, but while it's waxing, the solid edge of its shape will still fit into your cupped right hand. This is the logical time to perform any spellwork in which "increase" is an overall theme.

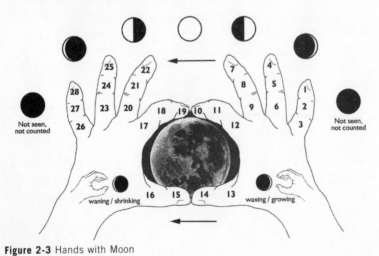

Figure 2-3 Hands with Moon

When the Moon reaches its first quarter—we see it as half-lit—it is directly to the South and overhead at sunset. You can point your right hand toward the setting sun and your left hand up to the overhead Moon, as if shaping a "three o'clock" position. When counting on your fingers, you can use this as a checkpoint in your count: You should be on your middle finger, but your count may have gotten a late start if the New Crescent wasn't visible for its first few days.

As it approaches full, the Moon is so far to the left of the Sun that it's rising in the East as the Sun's already lowering in the West. Finally, on the night of the Full Moon, the Sun sets as the Moon rises: Sunset and moonrise are fairly simultaneous. You'll have counted through all the right-hand fingers and out onto the right thumb. Hold the left hand up to meet the right, thumb-to-thumb and forefinger-to-forefinger, echoing the shape of the Full Moon as you "pass" it from right hand to left.

The count continues on the left hand as the Moon wanes. Once past full, the Moon is narrower each night and rises after the Sun has already set. Now the Moon's solid edge is caught in the C-shaped curve of your left hand. This is the time for spellwork in which "decrease" is your underlying theme, that is, banishing bad habits, getting closure, defining limits. As you come to the left little finger in your count, the now-tiny Moon-sliver will be rising just before dawn. The Moon has gone nearly full circle and is now just to the right of the Sun.

We can only count to 28 in this manner, but that's okay, because for at least a day or two the Moon is so closely in line with the Sun that we can't see it anyway. We won't begin counting again until the Moon reappears at sunset as a new Diana's Bow, the super-slender crescent seen low in the western sky.

So here is a new "rule of thumb," easy to remember, since to create the Full Moon's circle with our hands, we need to use the thumbs:

- Little fingers, little Moon (think of that tiny "fingernail clipping" shape).
- Thumb joints, Full Moon—either almost, exactly, or just past.
- *Widdershins* means right to left, moon-wise, opposite the Sun's motion, so:
- Right-hand backward-C-shape, the Moon is waxing, growing larger.
- Left-hand C-shape, the Moon is waning, shrinking in size.

The Moon's Unseen Phases

If you're using a calendar that supplies more information than just a black circle to mark the New Moon, or if you're using an ephemeris (a symbol-laden guide to the daily placement of all the planets), the glyphs and time shown will tell you when the Moon is precisely conjunct the Sun. That info generally looks something like this:

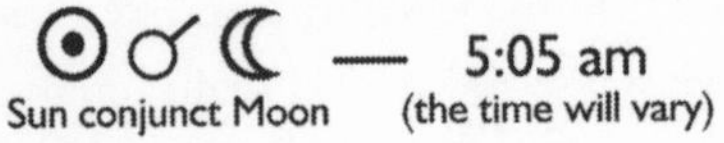

☉ ☌ ☾ —— 5:05 am
Sun conjunct Moon   (the time will vary)

Figure 2-4 Ephemeris information sample

This probably doesn't mean 5:05 A.M. (or whatever) in your own time zone, so be prepared to make simple corrections, as if figuring the time difference for a long distance phone call.

Dark: The Moon is considered "dark" when it's no longer visible as a tiny waning crescent in the early morning but hasn't yet reached its exact conjunction. Up until our hypothetical 5:05 A.M., the Moon is still waning, and its energy is still symbolically lessening. Any waning-Moon spellwork is apropos.

New: Once the Moon reaches exact conjunction it's considered "new" (what I call "calendar new") even though it's not yet visible. This is waxing, "increase" energy, very fresh, a birthing time of new beginnings, good for launching new projects.

Using either Dark or New Moons will depend on knowing the exact time of the Sun-Moon conjunction. Some people are able to sense the shift of energies from Dark to New. If you intend to work at these times, make it personal: Practice attuning yourself to feel that shift. Or you may find you prefer to wait until you physically see Diana's Bow in the evening sky, and make that personal connection with the Moon a part of your working.

Experiment: Try varying times and phases to find what's most effective for you.

CHAPTER 3

Measurements

Nowadays, we tend to operate in either inches or metric, but what else might we use to measure something?

Ourselves. We can each use our body's own dimensions to delineate space.

This isn't a new idea. When you've added a pinch of spice to a recipe or paced off a room to "guesstimate" the size, you've used yourself as a measuring device. Over the centuries, this practice has been standardized to create the official measurements we use today, but the original versions were far more flexible. All are highly portable, since you aren't lugging along separate measuring tools. We're looking for personalized humanization here, not precise scientific standards. Here are a few examples:

What we call a "foot" was originally based on the length of someone's foot. Why not use your own? Maybe not for buying fabric or dealing with architects, but there's no reason we can't use our own foot-length in a metaphysical context. Take 5 heel-to-toe steps in each of the four directions from a center point. From one "corner" to the next will be 7 heel-to-toe steps, and when you connect those four corners with straight lines, the resulting square will measure 28 footsteps around the edges.[1] *(See Figure 3-1.)* Whether used as a square or curved outward into a circle, 28 reminds us of the Moon phases, a worthy underpinning to any magical space.

"Hands" are used to measure the height of a horse, from the ground to the withers. Officially that means 4 inches, which is likely to be close to the

Figure 3-1 Circle of steps

actual width of your hand, flat-palm-plus-thumb. Rather than using a measuring cup, a cupped hand can measure substances. In fact, some old recipes are written this way, calling for a "handful" of an ingredient.

Held up to the sky at arm's length, our hands can measure space itself. A single finger is a bit shy of 2°, the four fingers together equal about 7°, and the flat-palm-plus-thumb "hand" now represents 10° of sky. *(See Figure 3-2.)*

A "span" is the measurement of your hand with thumb and fingers widely extended. In a workshop on Celtic tree magic, we each used our personal hand-span to determine the length of our divining sticks. In some traditions, one selects or crafts an *athame* (a ritual knife used by many Wiccans to mark off ceremonial space, among other uses) with a blade equal in length to one's hand span. Held up to the sky, the fully extended thumb-to-pinkie handspan is about 20°, and the mildly stretched thumb-to-forefinger about 15°. *(See Figure 3-3.)*

A "fathom" is used nautically to measure the water's depth. Watch any good pirate flick and you'll see some nameless swabby drop a weighted line over the side and then measure the cord—across his chest with arms fully extended—as he pulls the line back in. The dictionary defines a "fathom" as 6 feet, but a Greek source from 450 BCE cites the fingertip-to-fingertip fathom as 7 feet.[2] Which is correct? Both. Six feet is the modern official fathom. But when friends and I took our personal foot- and fingertip to fingertip measurements, each of us found our own "personal fathom": The distance from fingertip to fingertip is equal to the length of one's own foot multiplied by 7, and often

7°

10° of sky-space, or one "hand"

Figure 3-2 Flat hand

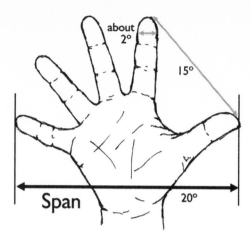

about
2°

15°

Span

20°

Figure 3-3 Hand Span

exactly equal. The 28-footstep square we saw in *Figure 3-1* measures 4 personal fathoms around its borders.

Another ancient unit of measurement was the cubit. The word comes from the Latin *cubitum*, which means "elbow": This is a measurement from your elbow to the tip of your middle finger. You may find, as I did, that two of your hand spans are equal to your own cubit. In ancient Egypt, the "royal cubit" was based on the fingertip-to-elbow measurement of the pharaoh, and the measurement probably changed slightly from one reign to the next. In the Louvre Museum in Paris, a beautiful measuring rod from the reign of Amenhotep I (1559–1539 BCE) shows his personal royal cubit to be 20.67 inches.[3] In some traditions, one selects or crafts a wand equal in length to one's personal cubit. In my shamanic practices, my frame drum serves as an ideal Zero-circle "portal," and the beater I use with my drum is 1 cubit long.

Personal measurements provide an opportunity to be wildly creative. If you're doing a spell for mental clarity, find a way to incorporate your head measurement. If your spellwork is aimed at expressing your feelings more clearly, try incorporating the distance from your heart to your mouth. Talismans, charms, garments, and tools: When we personalize these items, we imbue them with powerful ties to our own imaginations, associations, bodies, and beliefs.

CHAPTER 4

The Days of the Week

Only five real planets were known to the ancients: Mercury, Venus, Mars, Jupiter, and Saturn.[1] The other two celestial lights, the Sun and the Moon, aren't planets: Our Sun is a star and the Moon is Earth's natural satellite. However we define them now, the long history of 7 as a magical number comes largely from these seven shifting sky-objects (*See Figure 4-1*), and their number didn't change until Uranus was discovered in 1781. Humans have watched those seven easily visible objects for many millennia, and we watch them still. For simplicity's sake, we'll refer to them all as "planets" in this chapter.

The word *planet* comes from the Greek word *planetai*, meaning "wanderers." Each of these celestial bodies can be tracked moving through the sky along the slim band of space also occupied by the twelve astrological constellations. As if watching giant storybook illustrations, Earth's ancient peoples saw the planets move across the sky, meeting with and parting from each other while making their orbital journeys, always with the zodiac's fixed stars—the "firmament"—as their backdrop. Besides sparking our inspiration for astronomy, astrology, sky watching, and a world's worth of myths and creation tales, these seven sky-travelers inspired our calendar.

Different areas of influence were attributed to each deity and each planet, and because there were seven planets, we have a 7-day week. This is old, old, old: The Babylonians assigned gods and planets to the same 7-day

The Sun doesn't truly move anywhere —we orbit it. Many of our ancestors actually were aware of this, at least during some periods of history. However, Earth's own motion around the Sun causes the backdrop of constellations behind the Sun and the other planets to constantly shift as seen from our earth-bound perspective. Because it's orbiting us and we're rotating, too, the Moon's backdrop against the zodiac changes most rapidly. The Moon enters a new sign, a new constellation, about every 2.25 days.

Figure 4-1 Sun Sidebar

week still found on our calendars.[2] Maybe it just seemed fair that each deity should rule over his or her own day. Since the days and their traditional themes impact our magical use of numbers and often influence our decisions about when to perform various types of spellwork, they merit closer attention.

First Day of the Week: Sunday

Dies solis (Latin), *domingo* (Spanish), *dimanche* (French), day of the Sun

The Sun is our most prominent "planet," the star that gives its name—Sol—to our solar system. It dominates our daytime hours, and its absence creates our night. Its larger motions regulate our seasons.

The Babylonians knew the Sun as Shamash. To the Sumerians, he was Uttu; to the Persians, Mithra; and to the Egyptians, Ra or Re. To the Greeks, he was Hyperion ("dweller on high") and later Helios. To the Romans, the Sun was Sol, or Apollo. These are all male identities. In the same way some of us habitually call every dog "he" and every cat "she," many of us personify the Sun as masculine.

Plenty of civilizations have seen this differently. In early Egypt, Hathor was associated with the Sun: Her headdress was a bright red solar disk nestled between cow horns, and some texts call her the "eye of the Sun." Hathor's main temple was in Dendera, a vast complex with rooms available for physicians who healed using trance and the hot springs sacred to Hathor. She was also the Lady of the West, where she disappeared each night, heating the waters of all the hot, sacred springs while out of sight below the Earth.[3]

By the various names Sul, Sulis, and Sulis Minerva, our closest star was also a goddess to the British; she ruled over hot springs and healing waters there, too.[4] If the connection to water seems surprising, consider that many of Britain's sacred springs have a high iron content, making the waters run red, like hot birth—waters flowing from Mother Earth Herself.[5] If you've soaked in a natural hot spring—sacred sites wherever they are found, whatever color their water—you know that even in winter on the grayest days, you emerge feeling reborn, as if internally sun-heated.

The Sun is female elsewhere as well. Saule—her Baltic name—is another Sun goddess, as is Solntse, the identity by which she's known to the Slavic peoples.[6] To early Germans, she was Sunnu or Sunna—the origin of our own word for this star—and each day started when she awoke and began spinning light.[7] The Japanese call her Amaterasu, and her round red face is still the symbol on their flag.

Because of the Sun's role as light-bringer, illumination is a Sunday theme in magical workings. That bright gleam can relate to the radiant glow of health, the sparkle of monetary wealth, or a leap into the spotlight. Small wonder that we've come to associate the Sun with success, vitality, and abundance. Since each new day begins with the Sun's reappearance at dawn, Sunday is also thematically associated with both new beginnings on entirely new endeavors, and with fresh starts and renewed energy for projects that may have stalled.

Topics appropriate to the Sun's day are also those concerning authority, fame, self-confidence, and courage. This could be the right time to focus on your leadership abilities, whether that means looking for them, refining or defining them, or putting them to use. Start new projects or reinvigorate old ones, appreciate or improve physical health, or answer ambition's call. Sunday is a prime time to do spells for career advancement and to call success or physical healing into your life.

The Sun

Numbers: 1 (day in the week) and 6 (Square of the Sun)

Goddesses: Aditi (Hindu), Amaterasu (Japanese), Bast (Egyptian), Brigid (Celtic), Brunissen (Celtic), Eos (dawn, Greek), Grianne

(Irish), Hathor (Egyptian), Igaehindvo (Cherokee), Malina (Pacific Rim Arctic), Nahar (ancient Syrian), Sekhmet (Egyptian), Shapash (Sumerian), Sul, Sulla, or Sulis (British), Sunna (Germanic), Syrya (Hindu), Suwa (Arabian), Ushas (dawn, Hindu), Wakahiru-me (rising, Japanese), the Yatudhanis (Hindu) [8,9]

Gods: Amun-Ra (Egyptian), Apollo (Greco-Roman), Babbar (early Sumerian), Baldur (Scandinavian), Bochica (Colombian), Byelbog (Slavonic), Chango (African-Caribbean), Dharme (Hindu-Bengali), Dyaus (Hindu), Evua (Guinean), Helios (Greek), Hermakhis (rising or setting, Egyptian), Hiruku (Japanese), Huitzilopochtli (Aztec), Hun-Ahpu-Vuch (Guatemalan), Hyperion (early Greek), Inti (Incan), Kinich-Ahau (Mayan), Legba (Haitian voudoun), Lugh (Celtic), Mandulis (Nubian), Mao (Benin), Marduk (Babylonian), Maui (Polynesian), Melkart (Phoenician), Mithra (Persian), Mitra (Hindu), Orunjan (midday sun, Nigerian Yoruban), Päivä (Finno-Ugric), Perun (Slavonic), Punchau (Incan), Ra (Egyptian), Sabazius (Thracian/Phrygian), Shamash (Babylonian), Sol (Roman), Surya (Hindu), Tezcatlipoca (Aztec), Tlalchitonatiuh (afternoon sun, Aztec), Tonatiuh (Aztec), Torushompek (Brazilian Tupi-Guarani tribes), Upulero (Indonesian), Uttu (Sumerian), Vaseduva (early Hindu), Vishnu (Vedic Hindu) [9,10]

Element: Fire

Metal: Gold

Stones: Amber, carnelian, citrine, diamond, garnet, ruby, sunstone, tiger's eye, golden topaz

Herbs: Angelica, bay, chamomile, eyebright, frankincense, heliotrope, juniper, marigold, rosemary, rue, saffron, St. John's Wort, sunflower

Trees:[11] Birch, broom, or wild acacia

Tone:[12] Re—D

Colors: Gold, orange, yellow, red

Astrological Sign: Leo ♌

Diameter: 865,000 miles

Mean distance from Earth: 92.96 million miles

Earth's time to orbit the Sun: 365.25 days

Second Day of the Week: Monday

Monandæg (Old English), *dies lunae* (Latin), *lunes* (Spanish), *lundi* (French), Moon's day

Monday takes its name from the Moon. We may veer away from thinking of the Moon as male, but many cultures had no problem with that concept. The Moon was the male deity Sin to the Babylonians. To the Japanese, he's Tsukiyomi, brother of Amaterasu. The Hopi call the Moon the "Foolish Man Who Runs Around with No Home."[13]

However, many other cultures saw the Moon as female, and the list of her names is never ending. One of the most familiar is Luna, which was both the Latin word for "moon" and one of many names for the Roman moon goddess. The word *lunate*, meaning "crescent-shaped," comes from Luna. So do *lunacy* and *lunatic.* These words once referred to ecstatic devotees of the Moon, but they're now used more pejoratively: *Loony* traces its roots back to Luna.

Much of the folklore surrounding the Moon focuses on the planet's wandering nature and shape-shifting looks. Luna is traditionally associated with psychic and magical concerns, and with our human longings to shift our own energies as gracefully as the Moon seems to shift hers. The Moon is also associated with female fertility. That connection comes from the similar lengths of lunar cycle and menstrual cycle, and the shape-changing nature of pregnancy. Honoring their connection with the forces of Nature, many women now refer to their menstrual periods as their "Moon-time." The poetic "I'm on my Moon" is a marked improvement over the often derogatory terminology of times past.

Cultures throughout the world tracked the Moon and noted her cycles and her shifting placement, sometimes encrypting this information into the alignments of their architecture, and continually depicting her in art. This is certainly an indication of how much the Moon mattered to them. She sheds light on our dark nights, making the Moon a poignant symbol of inner light—enlightenment—as well. Whether or not the all ancients knew that moonlight is reflected sunlight, old lore is rife with references to moonlight itself reflecting, often on water. Reflected sunlight presents a blinding glare; reflected moonlight is beautiful, bright but soothing, and helps fuel the Moon's poetic associations with duality, mirrors, reflections, and illusiveness. Catch some moonlight in water, to drink or add to a bath, as a way of immersing yourself in Luna's magic.

Do your own sensibilities shift with the phases of the Moon, or with its presence in various signs of the zodiac? You might have days when you're less able to focus in a disciplined manner, nights with more vivid dreams, periods of more active imagination or bursts of creative fervor . . . or a lack of those experiences. If you find a lunar-related pattern, why not use it to your own advantage: Avoid detail work when you're apt to be in creative overdrive, and save boring tasks for times when your imagination is likely to be muted. If you keep a journal, sketch the Moon's current shape—from observation, not from copying a calendar—as a way to heighten your awareness of her changes. Use your connection to the Moon cycle as a means to acknowledge your connection with the forces of Nature as your own creative energies ebb and flow.

The Moon's own day is appropriate to any work involving imagination, dreams, or psychic knowledge. It's also well attuned to issues of emotional health and healing. Not surprisingly, the Moon's day is also associated with magical questions of childbirth and female fertility. (For male fertility, see Saturday.)

The Moon

Numbers: 3 (lunar phases: waxing, full, and waning) and 9 (Square of the Moon)

Goddesses: Aine of Knockaine (Irish), Al-Lat (Arabian), Anumati (waning Moon, Hindu), Arianrhod (Full Moon, Welsh), Artemis (Greek), Auchimalgen (Chilean), Belili (Sumerian), Bendis (Thracian/Phrygian), Brigid (Celtic), Brizo (Greek), Callisto (Greek),

Ceridwen (Welsh), Ch'ang-o (Chinese), Chia (Colombian), Coatlicue (Aztec), Cybele (Greek), Cynthia, Diana (Roman), Gungu (New Moon, Hindu), Hagar (Hebrew), Hecate (Greek), Hun-Ahpu-Myte (Guatemalan), Hunthaca (Colombian), Ida (Hindu), Io (Greek), Ix Chel (Mayan), Jarah (New Moon, Hebrew), Ka-ata-killa (pre-Incan), Komorkis (Blackfoot), Kuhu (New Moon, Hindu), Luna (Roman), Mama Quilla (Incan), Mari (Basque), Meztli (Aztec), Mylitta (Assyro-Babylonian), Oshun (New Crescent, African-Caribbean), Oya (Dark Moon, African-Caribbean), Phoebe (Greek), Raka (Full Moon, Hindu), Re (Phoenician), Sams (Semitic), Sefkhet-Seshat (Egyptian), Selene (Greek), Sina (Polynesian), Sinvali (New Moon, Hindu), Sirdu (Chaldean), Tanit (Carthagian), Telita (Babylonian), Xochiquetzal (Aztec), Yemaya (Full Moon, African-Caribbean)[8,9]

Gods: Aah (early Egyptian), Alignak (Eskimo), Baiame (Australian Aborigine), Chandra (Hindu), Enzu (Chaldean), Fadu (Polynesian), Gou (Benin), Ilmaqah (Semitic), Itzamna (Mayan), Jacy (Brazilian tribal), Jarah (Semitic, as New Moon), Khonsu (Egyptian), Mah (Persian), Mait' Carrefour (Haitian), Mani (Nordic), Menu (Lithuanian), Metzli (Aztec), Myestas (Slavonic), Nanna (Sumerian), Osiris (Egyptian), Sin (Babylonian), Tsukiyomi (Japanese), Yarikh (Canaanite)[9,10]

Element: Water

Metal: Silver

Stones: Aquamarine, beryl, coral, emerald, moonstone, pearl, sapphire, selenite

Herbs: Almond, cucumber, jasmine, melons, mugwort, myrtle, poppy, purslane, seaweed, water lily, white sandalwood, wintergreen

Tree:[11] Willow

Tone:[12] Ti—B

Colors: Silver, violet, lilac. Also white (New), red (Full, for its connections with menstruation, birth, and the Full Moon's color during eclipse) and black (Dark)

Astrological Sign: Cancer ♋

Diameter: 2,160 miles

Mean distance from Earth: 240,000 miles

Synodic period (cycle in relation to Sun): 29 days, 12 hours, 44 minutes

Sidereal period (complete cycle of the zodiac): 27 days, 7 hours, 43 minutes

Third Day of the Week: Tuesday

Tiwesdæg (Old English), *Tiw's day* (Anglo-Saxon). *Martes* (Spanish), *mardi* (French), Mars' day

One of the earliest names for the god and planet Mars was Nergal, which is what the Babylonians called him. There, he ruled war and the Underworld, and was married to Ereshkigal, the Queen of the Underworld. Since war inevitably helped populate the Underworld, these two make a suitable—but ominous—match.

To the Thracian Greeks, he was Ares, god of war. Ares loved conflict and combat. Disgusted by his nonstop, gratuitous violence, the other gods barely tolerated him, with a few key exceptions. His twin sister Eris— "Strife"—obligingly provoked new battles on his behalf. Aphrodite was married to Ares' brother Hephaestus, but couldn't resist the original bad boy and bore Ares several children. And Hades, Lord of the Underworld, was appreciative of all the warrior-souls that Ares delivered.

His Roman name at first was Mamurius, and his identity was that of an erotic sheepherding deity. Son of Juno, fathered by a flower, he gradually became Mars, god of all vegetation and growth itself, the Roman god of agriculture. His eponymous month was March, time of the Spring Equinox, which was once the start of the calendar year. Traditionally the season to plant crops, March also became the preferred time to march away to war. As Rome became more militarized, Mars ruled both activities.[14]

The color red has a long association with Mars. The planet can appear red or an intense light orange. We use the phrase "seeing red" to express anger, and of course blood is red, from iron-rich hemoglobin. Mars' metal is iron, which responds to magnets, so there's an implicit image of magnetic attraction, mysterious, invisible, and potentially overpowering. Trying to attract something? Spells done using magnets and iron as symbolic objects are excellent uses of Mars' energies.

Matters change a bit in the northern lands. Tiw (Norse), Zui (South German), or Tyr (Scandinavian-Teutonic): By whichever name, he's a Scandinavian lawgiver . . . and war god. One of his names, Things, means "council," as this god also governed councils of state.[15] The concept of councils and law was anathema to battle-crazy Ares, so this is a significant shift.

The martial associations for Ares tend to dominate our modern Mars lore. These themes are most benevolently expressed as taking action, initiating change, seeking victory and achievement, and expending our strength and energy. Most of us never have to declare war, but we may have to pick the right day for assertive action.

But we can also reclaim the assertive and sexy spring energies of Mamurius, or focus on the Norse god Tiw for lawgiving and counsel. Use Tiw's day to bring group energies together for decision making, or channel Mars' will-power-energy into unified group will. That's ideally what "lawgiving" is, anyway: a people's agreement to behave in a specific manner for the common good. To this we might join Mars' earlier ties to agriculture and that magical spark of life that brings vibrant growth to plant life. Again, we have an image of assertive energies productively united.

Other benevolent applications of that combustible Mars energy include matters involving machinery, vehicles, and commercial cooking, so spellwork in these areas is apropos now.[16] (For domestic and romantic cookery, see Friday and Venus.)

Tuesday is a traditional day to do blessings and protection spells for cars and machines, and is equally appropriate to use for spells concerning restaurants, kitchens, forges, new gardens, and other places where the useful energies of Mars are needed.

The Planet Mars

Numbers: 2 (duality, opposition, sounds like Tiw), 3 (day in the week), and 5 (Square of Mars)

Goddesses: Anath, Bhumi (Hindu, mother of planet Mars), Brigid, Maeve, Morrigan[8,9]

Gods: Ares (Greek), Chango (African-Caribbean), Heracles (Greek), Mamurius (Roman), Mars (Roman), Nergal (Babylonian), Tyr (aka Tiw, Tui, Zui, Scandinavian-Teutonic)[9,10]

Element: Fire

Metals: Iron, steel

Stones: Agate, amethyst, bloodstone, carnelian, flint, garnet, red jasper, lodestone, onyx, pipestone, rhodochrosite, rhodonite, ruby, topaz, rubellite (red tourmaline)

Herbs: Basil, dragon's blood, garlic, ginger, mustard, nettle, onion, radish, red pepper, tarragon, tobacco

Trees:[11] Holly (red berries), kerm oak (Kermes beetles, a source of red dye, live on these oaks)

Tone:[12] Do—C

Colors: Red, scarlet

Astrological Signs: Aries ♈ and (with Pluto) Scorpio ♏

Diameter: 4,223 miles

Mean distance from Sun: 141.6 million miles

Time to orbit the Sun: 687 days

Fourth Day of the Week: Wednesday

Wodnesdæg (Old English), Woden's day. *Miércoles* (Spanish), *mercredi* (French), Mercury's day

First, he was Nabu, a Babylonian god. To the Greeks he was Hermes, and to the Romans, Mercury, the name we know now. Among true planets—which rules out the Moon—Mercury is the fastest-moving in its orbit, circling the Sun in a sprightly 88 days. Mercury never wanders far from Sol—no further than 28° away—and is only visible briefly in the East before dawn or briefly in the West after sunset, as if darting from one side of the Sun to the other. From this came the portrayal of deity Mercury as the gods' quicksilver messenger, always close at hand, ready to do the Sun's bidding. What a loyal messenger!

The Roman Mercury was a cunning trickster from birth, and his exploits as a wee cattle-thieving baby are recounted by Homer. Shakespeare's original audiences got the implications of cleverness and caprice when Mercutio appeared in *Romeo and Juliet*. "Mercurial" comes from Mercury. So do the words *merchant* and *mercantile*, and merchants need clear wits and sharp people skills. Those on the opposite end of commerce come under Mercury's rule, too, since the need for cunning and speed made Mercury the god of thieves. It's more of that trickster energy again.

The divine messenger also rules travel, an association shared with the Greek wing-heeled Hermes, the god of the crossroads. In earlier times, road markers called herms stood at crossing points to guide and guard the way. Besides being markers, herms were wayside shrines, places to leave offerings and ask Hermes to grant swift, safe journeys. Blacksmiths might pay homage to Hermes as the "god of going."[17] (For Norse blacksmithing, see Thursday.)

Rome's young trickster Mercury ruled all music, having invented the lyre and the reed pipe. In American folklore, gifted blues musicians were purported to have met the devil at a crossroads and traded their souls for musical skill. Rhythm, drumming, and all percussion can come under Mercury's care as well, for the use of cadence in smithing, poetry and storytelling (communications again), and for the drum's long tradition of use in shamanic journeying, the "non-ordinary reality" form of travel.[18]

In myth and fairy tale, road crossings are places of change, choice, and superstition. In some cultures, the bodies of murderers and suicides were buried at crossroads, and executions sometimes took place there. Perhaps a crossroads location would hasten the souls' ultimate Crossing Over. That's because, along with his other tasks, Mercury-Hermes was a psychopomp, one who guides departing souls into the Afterlife, that Non-Corporeal Grand Tour that awaits us all. Woden, the chief Norse Æsir god, was a psychopomp for the honored dead, in addition to ruling over war, magic, poetry, cunning, gambling, and nocturnal weather. He was a favorite deity among rulers and warriors. Another Conductor-of-Souls was Tehuti, a.k.a. Thoth, the Egyptian psychopomp-god who also ruled over wisdom and writing (communications *again*). Was the psychopomp attribute an early metaphor for how departing spirits should "move toward the light" with help from the small planet that always stayed so near the Sun?

Themes apropos to Mercury's Day are all types of communications, including divination. Spells for eloquence can be done on Wednesdays, as can spells for travel protection, especially for business trips and any other journeys that must be prompt rather than leisurely. One might choose to conduct psychopomp work—encouraging departed souls to fully cross over—at this time. The old connections with cunning and wisdom also make Wednesday a fine time to focus your mental energies on study and creative thinking, or on business endeavors and the clear-cut goal of making sales. If your work is travel oriented, if you practice the old crafts of blacksmithing or poetry, if you drum or make other forms of music, pay special heed to this deity and day.

The Planet Mercury

Numbers: 1 (planet nearest the Sun), 4 (day in the week), and 8 (Square of Mercury)

Goddesses: Athena (Greek), Brigid (Irish), Ma'at (Egyptian), Metis (Greek), Rosmerta (Gaulish, consort of Mercury), Seshat (Egyptian)[8,9]

Gods: Anubis (Egyptian), Hermes (Greek), Elegba (African-Caribbean), Mercury (Roman), Nabu (Babylonian), Ogma (Irish), Tehuti or Thoth (Egyptian), Woden (Norse)[9,10]

Element: Air

Metals: Quicksilver, electrum (an alloy of gold and silver)

Stones: Agate, amber (in Latin, amber was called electrum, perhaps from its ability to produce sparks), aventurine, chrysoprase, emerald, hematite, jasper in mixed colors, opal, peridot, sapphire, turquoise

Herbs: Anise, caraway, dill, elecampane, fennel, fenugreek, horehound, lavender, licorice, mandrake, marjoram, mullein, pomegranate, valerian

Trees:[11] Ash, hazel, or almond

Tone:[12] Mi—E

Colors: Violet, yellow, multihued and variegated

Astrological Signs: Gemini ♊ and Virgo ♍

Diameter: 3,031 miles

Mean distance from Sun: 36 million miles

Time to orbit the Sun: 88 days

Fifth Day of the Week: Thursday

Thor's Day. *Donnerstag* (German) from Donner (thunder) for Thor the Thunderer. *Jueves* (Spanish), *jeudi* (French), Jove's day

The huge planet Jupiter is beautiful, slow, and stately, qualities that were interpreted as the human themes of abundance, judgment, and wisdom in the planet's associated deities. These traits echo through the gods' stories despite some all-too-human frailties.

As Bel, this planet was seen as a ruler by the Babylonians. Like so many deities, he was a vegetation-god, but he also was a god of air and of mountains. Jupiter (or Jove) was the supreme Roman deity. He ruled thunder and lightning, and indeed all weather. Many of his ancient temples are found on the high places, on hill- and mountaintop. Oaks, the tallest trees and those most prone to lightning strikes, were his. While these associations with air and the sky gave Jupiter some common points with Bel, they also caused Jupiter to gradually become equated with Zeus.

The early Zeus of Crete was a dying-and-regenerating vegetation god. The later Greek Zeus overthrew his domineering father, Cronus, but then assumed Cronus' heavy-handed traits. Zeus could be wise and just, but was also notorious for his predatory "amorous" assaults on mortal women and the occasional young boy. These tales are interwoven, convoluted, possibly mythic reflections of goddess cultures conquered by Zeus' devotees. Late tales emphasize the jealousy of Hera, Zeus' twin sister-wife, and her cruelty toward the women he raped, but in earlier versions, Hera was a husband-free pre-Hellenic Aegean earth goddess. Casting Zeus and Hera as twins was a way of saying they were equal, which likely was a demotion for her. *Hera* means "protectress," from her role as protectress of mortal women, but probably the name began as *He Era*, meaning "Earth."[19] A Babylonian birth-goddess, Erua, may be an earlier version of her.[20] However we now choose to sort this all out, it behooves us to be clear about the qualities we're invoking.

Meanwhile, Thor is the Norse god of the sky and thunder, bombastic yet benevolent toward humankind. In contrast to his warrior-father Woden, Thor was a god of the working classes, especially popular with sailors, farmers, and other weather-dependent folks. Thor's thunder and strength were equated with blacksmithing, which in this pantheon symbolized the forging of alliances. His hammer, Mjollnir, was both a tool and a weapon, a symbol of power used wisely, and his raven-companions, Hugin (Thought) and Munin (Memory), show access to knowledge of future and past. Thor's benevolence makes him easy to equate with Jupiter, who, by his other name—Jove—gives us the word *jovial*. The gods associated with Jupiter are generally viewed as kindly, generous, and good-natured. Community and the common good were among their early themes.

Thor's Day is considered to be good for spiritual growth (that lightning flash of insight), and practical matters like growth and material gain, especially through the expansion of existing enterprises. Convivial pursuits—community work and celebrations—are apropos, too. Since Thor, Jove, and early Hera look kindly on humans, this can be a good day to seek their blessing for wise decision making, or to pursue your most inspired ambitions. Climb mountains!

Thursday is also traditionally associated with issues of law and justice, and used for spellwork involving court cases. A caution here: Some interpretations of Jupiter and Zeus stress their overbearing tendencies. Few of us yearn for more authority figures in our lives. Why not redefine our concepts? Rather than equating them with Those Who Must Be Obeyed, try perceiving them instead as benevolent intercessors, or as sages and crones, the wise ones, elders and teachers who dwell quietly among us and within ourselves.

The Planet Jupiter

Numbers: 4 (Square of Jupiter) and 5 (day in the week)

Goddesses: Gaea, Isis (Egyptian), Hera (Greek), Juno (Roman supreme goddess, sister-spouse of Jupiter), Rhiannon, Themis (Greek)[8,9]

Gods: Bel (Assyrian-Babylonian), Jupiter (Roman), Llyr (British), Marduk (Assyrian-Babylonian), Obatala (African-Caribbean), Thor (Norse), Zeus (Greek)[9,10]

Elements: Air and Fire

Metal: Tin

Stones: Amethyst, carnelian, peridot, diamond, emerald, lepidolite, sapphire, sugilite, turquoise

Herbs: Agrimony, betony, borage, cinquefoil, dandelion, hyssop, mistletoe, nutmeg, sage

Trees:[11] Oak or terebinth

Tone:[12] Sol—G

Colors: Light and dark blues, purple

Astrological Signs: Sagittarius ♐ and (with Neptune) Pisces ♓

Diameter: 89,400 miles

Mean distance from Sun: 483.6 million miles

Time to orbit the Sun: 11.86 years

Sixth Day of the Week: Friday

Frigedæg (Old English), Freya's or Frigg's day. *Viernes* (Spanish), *vendredi* (French), Venus' day

The planet Venus was seen as the celestial manifestation of one of the earliest, most glorious goddesses of the ancient world: Inanna. Poetry written on her behalf still sings with the beauty, sensuality, hope, and excitement that her planet inspired in the ancient Sumerians. Along with love, she ruled fertility: Plants and grains pour from her womb, the orchards flourish, game is plentiful, plants fill the meadows.[21] Her periods of visibility are roughly equal to the length of a woman's pregnancy.

The planet that provoked ecstatic verses even 5,000 years ago still inspires us. Second out from the Sun, between Mercury and Earth, Venus never gets far from Sol—47° max—so she's catching the Sun's light from up close. Also, Venus is shrouded in clouds, which help to brilliantly reflect sunlight toward us awestruck Earthlings. She is by turns our Morning Star and our Evening Star. Earlier civilizations noted both of Venus' appearances and, in some cases personified them as two different deities. We shouldn't assume from this that they thought they were looking at two different planets: Many simply gave distinguishing names and qualities to each appearance.

Venus' ancient symbol among the Sumerians was an eight-pointed star or "rosette." This expresses the eight-year cycle during which Venus draws her pentacle (as we'll see in Chapter 10), and can refer to her roughly eight months of visibility, whether as Evening or Morning Star. It's also a graphic depiction of her elongation, her separation from the Sun. The actual elongations range from 45° to 47°, with an average of 46°. A circle divided into 45° segments will yield eight pieces, just as Venus' eight-petalled rosette shows.

The Romans called her Venus. For them, she ruled Nature's wild places, plants and creatures, and the fertility and health of all these. Eventually Venus merged with Greek Aphrodite, ruler of all sexuality, especially the human emotions and senses. In many versions of her myth, sea foam-born Aphrodite first landed on the isle of Cyprus. The island's copper mines are ancient and provide the Venus connection to both copper and the color green, since aging copper takes on a rich green patina called "verdigris."

She was also Freya, the Great Mother-Goddess in the northern pantheon, where she is queen of all plant and animal life, of sexuality, *seidh* (shamanic vision) and magic. Mighty Woden went to Freya to learn magic. Woden's own wife Frigg ruled over domestic creative skills, food, clothing, and the maternal expressions of love. In some late versions of the mythology, the identities of Freya and Frigg were merged.

Whether honoring Freya, Inanna, Aphrodite, or Venus, Friday is associated with love and passion, harmony, beauty, fertility, and the arts. Good times, camaraderie, anything that brings pleasure or sensual delight is appropriate to her day. It's the preferred time for spells to call forth romance, and the traditional day on which to invoke creativity in artistic or sensory pursuits—music, food, visual arts, the arts of love, humor, dance—or to celebrate the joy of these endeavors.

And we can use Friday to honor our struggles in these areas, too. What do we learn through love in all its forms, all its faces? In our most intimate interactions, those of the heart—family, friends, lovers, acts of creation and passion, personal truths, conscience—we can find profound teachings, ones we spend a lifetime learning to understand and embrace. Spells to comprehend these challenges are good work for Venus' day.

The Planet Venus

Numbers: 5 (Venus' pentacle orbit), 6 (day in the week), and 7 (Square of Venus)

Goddesses: Al-Uzza (Arabian), Anunet (Sumerian), Aphrodite (Greek), Astarte (Canaanite), Attar (as Morning Star, Arabian), Belit-Ilanit (as Evening Star, Chaldean), Beltis (Assyro-Babylonian), Chasca (Incan), Dennitsa (as Morning Star, Slavonic), Freya (Teutonic), Frigg (Teutonic), Gendenwitha (as Morning Star, Iroquois), Hathor (Egyptian), Inanna (Sumerian), Ishtar (Assyro-Babylonian), Isis (Egyptian), Mariamne, Mylitta (Assyro-Babylonian), Nu Chien (as

Morning Star, China), Oshun (African-Caribbean), Tethys (Greek), Vechernyaya (as Evening Star, Slovanic), Venus (Roman)[8,9]

Gods: Apisiharts (as Morning Star, Blackfoot), Dionysus (Greek), Eros (Greek), Hesperus (as Evening Star, "the western one," Greek), Min (Egyptian), Pan, Phosphoros (as Morning Star, "bringer of light," Greek), Ruda (as Evening Star, Arabian), Sahar (as Morning Star, Phoenician), Salem (as Evening Star, Phoenician), Tai-Po (as Evening Star, China), Tlahuizcalpantecuhtli (as Morning Star, Aztec)[9,10]

Element: Earth

Metal: Copper

Stones: Amber, azurite, beryl, chrysocolla, chrysoprase, coral, emerald, jade, green jasper, kunzite, lapis lazuli, malachite, olivine, pearl, peridot, ruby, sodalite, green tourmaline, turquoise

Herbs: Birch, mugwort, myrtle, orris root, pennyroyal, periwinkle, raspberry, rose, thyme, vervain, violet

Trees:[11] Apple or quince

Tone:[12] La—A

Colors: Green, rose pink, indigo

Astrological Signs: Taurus ♉ and Libra ♎

Diameter: 7,519 miles

Mean distance from Sun: 67.2 million miles

Time to orbit the Sun: 224.7 days

Seventh Day of the Week: Saturday

Dies Saturni (Latin), *sábado* (Spanish), *samedi* (French), Saturn's day

As the slowest moving of the planets known to the ancients, Saturn was often associated with old age, finality, and endings.

The planet Saturn was first identified as Ninib, a Babylonian deity who ruled the weather and Earth's fertility. As beliefs and practices migrated, he became Cronus to the Greeks and then Saturn to the Romans, sometimes confused with Chronos, "Father Time," mowing down life with his sickle, still seen in the shape of Saturn's astrological glyph. Robert Graves traces this sickle back to a crow's-bill-shaped hook used for reaping, especially any ritually performed cutting, as when mistletoe is lopped from an oak or the last grain stalk harvested. These are indeed endings, but endings that come with awareness, conscious of the future they inherently contain, like the seed heads in the mown grain.[22]

There are variations on Cronus' story, of course. In some versions, he's father-castrating Cronus, who protected his siblings and Mother Earth by cutting off father Uranus' genitals with a flint sickle and flinging them into the sea (something like cutting off the grain's seed head, but probably darn different to Uranus). Cronus became in turn another tyrant-father. Knowing from prophesies that one of his children with Rhea would depose him, Cronus swallowed all the babies at birth rather than risk their rivalry. Finally, with the help of Rhea herself, one child—Zeus—evaded Cronus' wrathful maw, grew to manhood and conquered Dad. Zeus tricked Cronus, all the devoured children were safely vomited forth, and Cronus was either slain or banished. One big happy family!

In other, earlier versions, Rhea was the important one, an independent Great Goddess, endlessly creating and destroying—significantly, she did both—until her myths were rewritten by conquerors who assigned Cronus as her domineering husband.

To the Romans, Saturn was a god of fertility and planting, but he was still connected to endings. His main ritual was the Saturnalia, a wild event held from December 17 to 23, culminating at the Winter Solstice, the end of the solar year. This massive celebration of the final days in Sol's southern journey was marked with feasts, presents, and wild role reversals, as slaves were served (briefly) by their masters.

In astrological terms, Saturn often deals with learning from life so we can move forward afresh instead of perpetually dragging that same old baggage along. Why wait 29.5 years for a Saturn return to grace (smite?) your birth chart when you can revisit the whole collection of karmic themes any Saturday?

This is a pretty mixed collection of associations, but finality is a constant theme. By moving so slowly through the zodiac, Saturn became the prototype of the venerable Father Time. Because the planet Saturn was believed to be at the ultimate outer edge of the universe, Saturday is at the end of the week. Endings again. Most benevolently, Saturday is considered a propitious time to deal with matters that concern boundaries, protection, and stability. Do spell-work to set limits, get closure, or bring something to a conclusion. This can be a time to cultivate your sense of patience and self-discipline: Holding ourselves in check is an expression of boundaries.

Saturday traditionally has ties to male fertility, but if you intend to use the day for this theme, you might prefer to focus on Saturn, Ninib, and the idyllic Cronus—farms, fertility, seeds, planting, and plenty—rather than the sad, mad, emotional-baggage-laden Cronus.

In memory of that gloomy Cronus, tragically stuck perpetuating a destructive multigenerational cycle, Saturdays can also be used to pursue greater understanding of large karmic issues. Spellwork to understand and heal family wounds and destructive cycles certainly wouldn't go amiss. This is brave and crucial work. What in your life needs some clear-eyed pruning to make room for the new?

The Planet Saturn

Numbers: 3 (Square of Saturn) and 7 (day in the week)

Goddesses: Ceres, Cybele, Demeter, Hecate, Hera, Isis (Egyptian), Kali (Hindu), Khaya (Hindu, mother of planet Saturn), Nephthys, the Norns, Rhea (Greek)[8,9]

Gods: Anubis (Egyptian), Baal (Phoenician), Bran (Manx/Welsh), Cronus (Greek-Phoenician), Ninib (Babylonian), Ogun (African-Caribbean), Saturn (Roman)[9,10]

Elements: Water and Earth

Metal: Lead

Stones: Apache tear, hematite, brown jasper, jet, obsidian, onyx, serpentine, star sapphire, schorl (black tourmaline), dravite (brown tourmaline), turquoise

Herbs: Asafoetida, Balm of Gilead, comfrey, cypress, hemlock, horsetail, ivy, juniper, mullein, nightshade, Solomon's Seal, valerian

Trees: Alder, poplar, yew, or pomegranate

Tone:[12] Fa—F

Colors: Indigo, black, green

Astrological Signs: Capricorn ♑ and (with Neptune) Aquarius ♒

Diameter: 74,980 miles

Mean distance from Sun: 886 million miles

Time to orbit the Sun: 29.5 years

Some Words of Advice

Now that I've mentioned all the swell and very ancient traditional reasons why you should use these days for particular affects, let me tell you why perhaps you shouldn't.

Many of these associations with planets and days are based on violent mythologies, often overlaid on mellower agrarian myths and deities. Yes, modern life still can be violent, but are there some aspects of these tales you'd rather not perpetuate? Most of us aren't particularly violent. Of course, most of us aren't particularly agrarian, either. So, maybe you decide to hone in on certain, very specific portions of the traditions, focusing on the counselor aspects of Tiw, for example, rather than on Ares' militant aspects. Good!

However, the whole point of picking a special time for your spellwork is to enhance your chances for successful results. Are the Higher Powers on the same seven-day week we use? Do they check their celestial day-planners and flunk us for picking the wrong day? Will thunder echo as a divine voice booms, "Request denied, lowly human!"?

Probably not. We use the various days symbolically to make the imagery more vivid for *ourselves*, not to appease cranky, clock-watching deities. Here on the earthly plane, authors don't come around to check that you're obeying their books (at least I don't). The path of neo-Wicca is one of personal responsibility and, as long as we "harm none"—including ourselves, other human beings, and all the rest of Mother Earth's children— we get to pretty much do what we want.

That said, I believe the Higher Powers respond to honest appeals that come from our hearts: "Please, help me!" If Fridays always feel cursed for you and Tuesdays always feel lucky, who cares what the books say? If your heart isn't in it, all the so-called correct days, colors, candles, and magical formulae on Earth won't help. So pick a day when your heartfelt plea can go out most clearly from *you*.

There's a well-intentioned and very strong human impulse to find (or try to impose) order in the Universe. When your intuition disagrees with that would-be orderly filing system, try trusting your intuition. At worst, a spell simply won't work as you envisioned—no lightning bolts are likely to smite you down. Remember, there are other reasons spells don't seem to work. By calling on Higher Powers for assistance, you're putting your trust in their vast, non-Earthbound perspective to deliver what you really need. Your heart's message will be clearly heard and responded to, though perhaps not in the precise way you envisioned. You have invoked Higher Powers: Their solutions tend to be far more creative than those we envision for ourselves.

Keep good records on all your spellwork, making note of what days you choose and why. These notes become your recipes for future work. Record your results as well. Your notes are your personal testimony: They serve as positive reinforcement and help validate this more spontaneous and intuitive method of working.

CHAPTER 5

The Magical Squares

We call them Magical Squares or Planetary Squares. Or Seals, or Kamea, or Tables. Like many magical tools, these are known by different names in different settings, but whatever name they go by, they date back hundreds—even thousands—of years. The earliest one on record, the 3-by-3 "order-3" square that we know as the Square of Saturn, is known in China as *Lo Shu*.

The Turtle and the Square of Saturn

Its discovery is credited to Emperor Yu the Great, the "Sage-King," circa 3000 BCE.[1,2] As he walked one day along the Lo River, a tributary to the mighty Yellow River, the emperor found a turtle. From the mysterious numerical designs on its back, Emperor Yu recognized that this was a magical creature, and he took it back with him to his palace. The turtle was venerated, and its sacred shell designs were studied with great delight by the court scholars.

According to this story of the turtle, what fascinated the Chinese court were unusual clusters of dots on the turtle's shell, odd-numbered groups in black and even-numbered groups in white. *(See Figure 5-1.)* The number sequence itself became the *Lo Shu*—Lo River Writing—which is mentioned in Chinese mathematical texts from circa 2200 BCE onward. Much later, in 1275 CE, mathematician Yang Hui wrote extensively about magic squares in his *Continuation of Ancient Mathematical Methods for Elucidating the Strange Properties of Numbers*. Yang Hui prefaced his book by saying that he was just passing along the work of earlier mathematicians. He didn't explain how most of his 3-, 4- and 5-order squares were designed, but he revealed a simple formula for constructing a *Lo Shu* square from scratch.[3] *(See Figure 5-2.)*

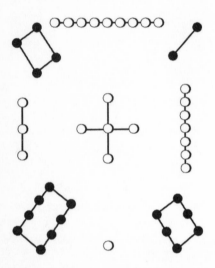

Figure 5-1 Turtle-shell pattern

A. **B.** **C.** **D.** **E.** 8 1 6

Figure 5-2 Building the *Lo Shu*. Write numbers 1 through 9 in three rows and tilt sideways to the right so 1 is up and 9 is down *(A)*. Switch positions of 1 and 9 *(B)*, and of 3 and 7 *(C)*. Bring the 9 down between 4 and 2 in top row *(D)*; pull 3, 5, and 7 together in second row, and bring the 1 up between 8 and 6 in bottom row *(E)*. Voilà!

For use as a magical square, we add gridlines between the numbers to create cells, but it's still the venerable *Lo Shu*. The eight outer groups of turtle-shell dots became the eight trigrams of the *I Ching*. *(See Figure 5-3.)* The *Lo Shu* are also familiar from *feng shui* work, where the nine positions are referred to as the "Nine Floating Stars," the basis for the *bagua*, the 3-by-3 grid pattern that determines the attributes and "cures" of *feng shui* space.[4] I've found little that clearly details the interwoven history back to that sacred turtle, but the *I Ching*, the Square of Saturn, the *Lo Shu*, and *feng shui* are all descended from that venerable animal.

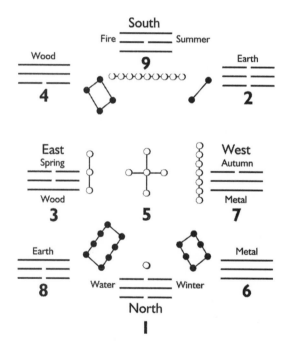

Figure 5-3 *I Ching/Lo Shu*

Playing with the Square of Saturn's Math

This is the smallest square and a good place to get a basic introduction to the workings and terminology. This little square is full of tricks, which just seem more amazing once you've seen how simply it was created.

First, this is an "order-3" square—that is, three cells across and three down—and contains numbers 1 through 9. A square's highest number should match the number of cells it contains.[5] (See Figures 5-4 and 5-5.)

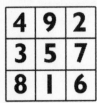

Figure 5-4 Square of Saturn

A.

B.

C.

Figure 5-5 Square of Saturn math

- Each row added across *(A)* equals 15, as does each column added top to bottom *(B)*.
- The corners added crosswise diagonally, upper left to lower right, and upper right to lower left *(C)*, will also total up to 15.
- If you add all the numbers in the square together— 1 + 2 + 3 + 4 + 5 + 6 + 7 + 8 + 9—the total is 45.
- Divide 45 by the square's order—3—and your result will be 15, same as each row total, column total, and diagonal total.

There's more:

- Add the pairs of numbers opposite each other. In the middle row, that's 3 + 7. Middle column is 9 + 1. The corners diagonally in pairs are 4 + 6, and 2 + 8. Each pair totals 10.
- Now, see the 5 in the center square, the one without a number to pair up with? Double the 5 by adding it to itself: 5 + 5. Total: 10, to match the edge-cell pairs. This will be true for the larger odd-order squares as well: Find the cell at dead center, double it, and then locate significant pairs throughout the square that match that sum.

Back to history. Did the *Lo Shu* square migrate out from China, or arise elsewhere independently?

Figure 5-6 Saturn with rosette

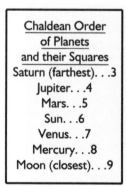

Figure 5-7 Scrying with the *Lo Shu*

Both. The Mayans were familiar with this square, as were northern Africans, and prehistoric French.[6] Ancient Babylonians united this square with the eight-point star of Ishtar to show the routes through it.[7] *(See Figure 5-6.)* One modern source offers a version of the square for crystal gazers: Draw the grid and its numbers on black paper with white chalk. The crystal ball is then placed in the center, where the 5 would normally be. *(See Figure 5-7.)* This version of the square is identified as an "Egyptian figure," so perhaps the Chinese turtle had an ancestor dwelling among the pharaohs.[8] Meanwhile, order-4 squares were known in India by circa 550 CE, when Varahamihira wrote a text called *Brhatsamhita* about divination. Some of Varahamihira's order-4 squares contained encoded recipes for perfume, while another was named *kacchaputa*, which translates as "the shell of a turtle," another link pointing back to the *Lo Shu* turtle, perhaps.[9]

Order-5 and -6 squares were known in Islamic lands by 983 CE. The *Qabs al-Anwar*, written by Nadruni about 1384 CE, listed the same seven planet-and-square pairings as shown in *Figure 5-8*, an arrangement reiterated by Pacioli's *DeViribus* in 1498, and again in Cornelius Agrippa's *De Occulta Philosophia* in 1531. This was known as the Chaldean order, and it matched each square's size with what was

Chaldean Order of Planets and their Squares
Saturn (farthest). . .3
Jupiter. . .4
Mars. . .5
Sun. . .6
Venus. . .7
Mercury. . .8
Moon (closest). . .9

Figure 5-8 Chaldean order

believed to be each planet's relative distance from the Earth: farther away, fewer cells. Closer, more cells.

Why would anyone think that the Sun is closer to Earth than Mars, Jupiter, and Saturn are? This actually wasn't such a foolish premise. The ancients watched the motions of the Moon, Mercury, and Venus: Sometimes each comes between Earth and the Sun; sometimes Mercury and Venus go behind the Sun. The Moon never does, so it must be the closest to Earth. By contrast, Mars, Jupiter, and Saturn *never* come between us and our star, but sometimes they pass behind the Sun as they circle, leading to the belief that they were farther away than Sol. Erroneous, but hardly foolish. Hence: the "Chaldean order," which still influences most magical number usage in the West. The tradition is long, the logic is short, so draw your own conclusions about whether and how to use the Chaldean order.

No order-2 square exists: A four-cell square can't do the requisite tricks of addition using numbers 1, 2, 3, and 4. Agrippa had a creative explanation for this: The number 2 was cursed through the actions of the first two humans, Adam and Eve, making an order-2 square impossible. This was also his "proof" that the four elements—Earth, Air, Fire, and Water, identified here with numbers 1 through 4—were inadequate. Agrippa *did* list an order-1 square—a single cell containing the numeral 1—which he assigned to God.[10] Perhaps this bizarre reasoning helped keep the Inquisition at bay.

Magic and Magical Squares

This is a good time to make a distinction: There are two kinds of squares, which we can call "magic" and "magical" to distinguish between them.

Magic squares are a form of "recreational mathematics," sort of like crossword puzzles for math buffs. They're called "magic" squares because their numbers can be added up in a variety of tricky ways. However, while the earliest versions were metaphysical, no mystical associations exist for most historical or contemporary magic squares. That's simply not their purpose, just like most crossword puzzles don't hold clues to the Akashic Record.

The second type, the truly *magical* squares, are similar in their math behavior, but they have the added attraction of very ancient roots and a long history of magical and occult uses. These are the ones we're interested in.

The Dürer Square (a.k.a. the Square of Jupiter, Almost)

Among the many people fascinated with magic/magical squares were artist Albrecht Dürer (1471–1528) and American statesman Benjamin Franklin (1706–1790). Franklin composed squares during periods of boredom in the Pennsylvania Assembly, where he served as clerk in the late 1730s, long before coming into his glory years as an elder statesman.[11] While both men probably relished the mental challenges of the squares, Franklin (who was a Freemason) and Dürer were certainly intrigued by the metaphysical aspects as well.

Figure 5-9 Durer's *Melencolia*

The Square of Jupiter appears in Dürer's print *Melencolia*—or nearly appears, since Dürer took liberties. *(See Figures 5-9, 5-10, and 5-11.)* Why use Jupiter's square when melancholy is metaphysically equated with the planet Saturn? Perhaps it was there as a cure: Jupiter (a.k.a. Jove, as in "jovial") was believed to counteract "saturnine" moodiness.

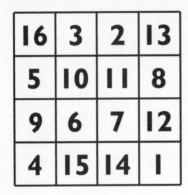

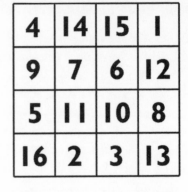

Figure 5-10 Dürer square

Figure 5-11 Square of Jupiter

Melencolia is loaded with occult references that art historians are still baffling over: a complex geometric solid, a seven-rung ladder, a compass (set to 51°25′, the measurement for crafting a seven-pointed star, or dividing a circle by 7) and other props. *(See Figure 5-11.)* We know Dürer enjoyed creating visual puzzles with which to challenge and amuse his friends, and *Melencolia* may have been one of these.

His decision to rotate the square 180° and otherwise alter it may have been sparked by the printing technique itself. In etching, an artist must create the entire composition as a mirror image of what the results will be, since the final print is the reverse of what's etched on the plate. That means any text or numbers must be written backward. As he worked out how to insert the numbers into his etching plate, did Dürer spot a chance to include the date? By rotating the layout of the traditional square, Dürer quietly hid the year—1514—in the bottom row. Another number—in reverse—isn't visible, although Dürer was certainly aware of it: Each Square of Jupiter row adds up to 34, and in 1514 Albrecht Dürer was forty-three years old.

We'll use Dürer's square to examine more things that some squares—magic or magical—can do. An order-4 square has sixteen cells, so the numbers contained are 1 through 16. Location, location, location—where each number is placed is crucial.

Playing with the Square of Jupiter's Math

Figure 5-12 shows the Square of Jupiter math.

- *A, B,* and *C*. Rows, columns, and diagonals as in the Square of Saturn. Each totals 34.
- *D*. As do the four corners themselves: 16 + 13 + 4 + 1 = 34, and
- *E*. The four center cells: 10 + 11 + 6 + 7 = 34.
- *F*. And even the pairs of inner numbers along facing edges:

3 + 2 + 15 + 14 (along the top and bottom edges) = 34
5 + 9 + 8 +12 (along the left and right edges) = 34

So far, that's fourteen different ways to add up to 34 in this square, but there are even more:

D and E. The four corners & the center squares = 34 each

F. Inner pairs on facing edges = 34 each way

G, H, I, J, K & L, shown below = 34 to each line combo

Figure 5-12 Square of Jupiter math

G, H, I, J, K, and *L* present another fourteen ways to reach 34 by adding together specific cells in the Jupiter square,[12] and there may be even more. Though *A, B,* and *C* are good in all the planetary squares, many of these other routes work in this square only. Not to fear, though, because other squares often do different tricks, which I leave it to you to discover if you find that this brain-game strikes your fancy.

So much for the crazy math. See the Bibliography for math-specific books if you crave more details, more squares, and more mentally challenging shapes.

Now let's get back to the mystical.

The Planetary Squares

Shown on pages 57 and 58 in order, from smallest to largest, the power of these squares isn't found by copying how they look; it's in the act of creating the square, from scratch, one number at a time. When you draw your own square, use the numbering sequence as a meditation. Inscribe each number in its proper order—1, 2, 3, and so on—within the square, rather than simply dashing them in row by row. *Hint*: Pencil the numbers in lightly first, then work with focused intention while inking them in—1 through whatever—in their proper order.

A couple of general notes:

First: If you multiple the center cell number from any odd-order square by the order-number itself, you'll find the row/column total for that square. For example, Mars is the order-5 square and its center number is 13, hence 5 x 13 = 65.[13]

Second: When its order is divisible by 3, a square's total will reduce to 9. All others reduce to 10 (and 1).

Third: All of the odd-order squares—Saturn, Mars, Venus, and the Moon—start in the same relative place. Locate the center square. Number 1 is directly below the center square, and the square's final number is directly over the center square. The central square itself will contain the "center" number: 1-2-3-4-**5**-6-7-8-9. Once you find the starting, mid-, and ending points, the pattern within these odd-order squares starts to reveal itself.

The even-order squares—Jupiter, the Sun, and Mercury—all begin with 1 in the upper right corner and end with their highest number in the lower left corner. Aside from that, their sequences are trickier, at least to my eye. Good luck finding their patterns!

Square of Saturn ♄

4	9	2
3	5	7
8	1	6

Figure 5-13 Square of Saturn

Use to enhance:
Understanding of past experiences
Developing personal discipline
Right use of limits and boundaries
Comprehension of karma
Refer to the material on Saturday in Chapter 4 for more [9]

Layout of Square: 3-by-3 grid, an order-3 square
Numbers contained:
1 through 9
Total for each row, column, and corner-to-corner diagonal: 15
Total for full square: 45
Order-number divided into total: 45 ÷ 3 = 15

Square of Jupiter ♃

4	14	15	1
9	7	6	12
5	11	10	8
16	2	3	13

Figure 5-14 Square of Jupiter

Use to enhance:
Success in legal cases
Business expansion
Good fortune, success (and your sense of joviality?)
Forging partnerships, alliances
Spiritual growth
Refer to the material on Thursday in Chapter 4 for more

Layout of Square: 4-by-4 grid, an order-4 square
Numbers contained:
1 through 16
Total for each row, column, and corner-to-corner diagonal: 34
Total for full square: 136
Order-number divided into total: 136 ÷ 4 = 34

Square of Mars ♂

11	24	7	20	3
4	12	25	8	16
17	5	13	21	9
10	18	1	14	22
23	6	19	2	15

Figure 5-15 Square of Mars

Use to enhance:
Taking action
Physical strength, energy
Personal courage and will power
Control of temper, passion
Blessings on vehicles and machinery
Mechanical aptitude
Commercial kitchens and cooking
Refer to the material on Tuesday in Chapter 4 for more

Layout of Square: 5-by-5 grid, an order-5 square
Numbers contained:
1 through 25
Total for each row, column, and corner-to-corner diagonal: 65
Total for full square: 325
Order-number divided into total: 325 ÷ 5 = 65

Square of the Sun ☉

6	32	3	34	35	1
7	11	27	28	8	30
19	14	16	15	23	24
18	20	22	21	17	13
25	29	10	9	26	12
36	5	33	4	2	31

Figure 5-16 Square of the Sun

Use to enhance:
Self-confidence
Health, vitality
Leadership abilities
Perception of goals
Self-actualization
Success in new projects
Refer to the material on Sunday in Chapter 4 for more

Layout of Square: 6-by-6 grid, an order-6 square
Numbers contained:
1 through 36
Total for each row, column, and corner-to-corner diagonal: 111
Total for full square: 666
Order-number divided into total: 666 ÷ 6 = 111

Square of Venus ♀

6	32	3	34	35	1
7	11	27	28	8	30
19	14	16	15	23	24
18	20	22	21	17	13
25	29	10	9	26	12
36	5	33	4	2	31

Figure 5-17 Square of Venus

Use to enhance:
Awareness of harmony
and beauty
Capacity for friendship
and love
Openness to joy, playfulness,
and romance
Inviting love and relationship
into your life
Sensory awareness
Domestic or sensual cookery
Refer to the material on Friday
in Chapter 4 for more

Layout of Square: 7-by-7
grid, an order-7 square
Numbers contained: 1
through 49
Total for each row, column,
and corner-to-corner
diagonal: 175
Total for full square: 1,225
Order-number divided into
total: 1,225 ÷ 7 = 175

Square of Mercury ☿

6	32	3	34	35	1
7	11	27	28	8	30
19	14	16	15	23	24
18	20	22	21	17	13
25	29	10	9	26	12
36	5	33	4	2	31

Figure 5-18 Square of Mercury

Use to enhance:
Clear thinking and perceptions
Articulate, effective
communications
Concentration, especially
for studying
Intellectual endeavors,
acquiring knowledge
Spirit plane communications
Safe and timely travel

Layout of Square: 8-by-8
grid, an order-8 square
Numbers contained:
1 through 64
Total for each row, column,
and corner-to-corner
diagonal: 260
Total for full square = 2,080
Order-number divided into
total: 2,080 ÷ 8 = 260

Square of the Moon ☽

6	32	3	34	35	1
7	11	27	28	8	30
19	14	16	15	23	24
18	20	22	21	17	13
25	29	10	9	26	12
36	5	33	4	2	31

Figure 5-19 Square of the Moon

Use to enhance:
Intuition and instinct
Fertility (be specific) and cre-
ativity
Emotional attunement
Psychic awareness
All gardening and farming
endeavors
Safe journeys involving water
Refer to the material on
Monday in Chapter 4 for more

Layout of Square: 9-by-9
grid, an order-9 square
Numbers contained:
1 through 9
Total for each row, column,
and corner-to-corner
diagonal: 369
Total for full square = 3,321
Order-number divided into
total: 3,321 ÷ 9 = 369

Using the Planetary Squares

Choose the planet whose traditional themes best match your concern. For example, to improve concentration while studying for a test, Mercury is a logical choice. Opening a new business is usually a Sun matter, while increasing trade at an existing business matches with Jupiter. Matters involving limits should be directed to Saturn. If you want blessings and protection for a new vehicle, Mars is the best choice.

A friend recently bought a diesel car that she's converting to run on recycled cooking oil. Brava! As a call to the goddess to keep the car and its occupants safe, we can choose a key word or short phrase: "Bless alt-fuel Mercedes" or "Protect my car" or perhaps "ABC-987," the (fictional) license plate number. For our purposes here, let's say, "Run well, be safe."

Next we find the numbers that correspond to the letters in our phrase. Our first option is to use a 1-through-9 key for the alphabet. *(See Figure 5-20.)* Many of us are probably familiar with this key already, since it's used in name numerology and simple ciphers.

Working from the 1-to-9 chart, our phrase looks like *Figure 5-21*.

1	2	3	4	5	6	7	8	9
A	B	C	D	E	F	G	H	I
J	K	L	M	N	O	P	Q	R
S	T	U	V	W	X	Y	Z	

Figure 5-20 Alphabet Key, 1 through 9

R U N   W E L L   B E   S A F E
9-3-5—5-5-3-3   2-5—1-1-6-5

Figure 5-21 "Run well, be safe," 1 through 9

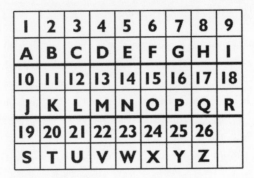

Figure 5-22 Alphabet Key, 1 through 26

If you're using the Saturn square or need letters *Q* through *Z* in the Jupiter square, you must use the 1-to-9 chart presented in *Figure 5-20*.

However, we're using the Mars square, an order-5 square with twenty-five individual cells. Since our phrase doesn't include *Z*, the twenty-sixth letter, we have another option: Instead of making the first nine numbers each do triple duty with the 1-to-9 chart, we can use a different number for each letter. To use unique numbers, use the 1-to-26 key presented in *Figure 5-22*.

Note: If you reduce each two-digit number, this chart will match the 1-to-9 chart in *Figure 5-20*.

Now our phrase looks like *Figure 5-23*.

R U N W E L L   B E S A F E
18-21-14—23-5-12-12   2-5—19-1-6-5

Figure 5-23 "Run well, be safe," 1 through 26

GEMATRIA

As we spell out different words, we sometimes find surprising numerical parallels between them. *Lion*, for example, is expressed in

---

numbers as 3-9-6-5; *cheetah* as 3-8-5-5-2-1-8; and *tiger* as 2-9-7-5-9, working with the simpler number chart *(Figure 5-20)*. With totals of 23, 32, and 32, respectively, all reduce to 5.

If you find this intriguing, gematria may be the study for you. Similar in practice to the feline example but far more complex, gematria is based on the twenty-two letters of the Hebrew alphabet, plus five of those same letters repeating in slightly different forms when they end a word, for a total of twenty-seven. Each letter is assigned a number value, but unlike the A-to-Z alphabets we've already seen, the values for these letters reach far higher—into the triple digits—so when each word is totaled, the sum can be hefty. Other differences: In gematria, the sums aren't reduced to single digits; each letter also has a deeper esoteric meaning; and, for many of us, the spelling must occur phonetically, since gematria's basis is Hebrew and many of us are working in English.

"The Kabalah calls the Hebrew alphabet the 'letters of the angels.'" So wrote Madame Blavatsky in *The Secret Doctrine*[14] and the use of those letters in gematria is one way of exploring their divine associations. Gematria is a deep, ancient, complex, and subtle study, and this is simply a very basic definition of the practice.

In gematria, the lion we met earlier becomes $30 + 10 + 70 + 50 = 160$, while the cheetah is a massive 60 *(ch)* $+ 8$ (the long e sound) $+ 300$ *(t)* $+ 1$ *(a)* $= 369$.

For deeper interpretations we would look to gematria's symbolic meanings. Here, through its letters, our obliging sample lion metaphorically consists of "ox-goad," "hand," "eye," and "fish."[15] *Lamed*, often translated "ox-goad," can in a larger sense mean something like "motivator." *Yod*, or "hand," can refer to how we translate our ideas into physical reality, grappling "hands on" with destiny. *Ayin*, or "eye," implies both what we see and what we understand: vision and perception, sight and insight. Finally, *Nun*, or "fish," might speak to an environment inhospitable to humans—what adjustments must we make to survive in hostile surroundings? Through these deeper meanings, the lion becomes a far more complex symbol.

Hebrew Name	Basic Meaning	Letter	Value
Aleph	cattle	A	1
Beth	house	B	2
Gimel	camel	C/G	3
Daleth	door	D	4
Heh	window	E/H	5
Vav	doorknob or nail	St/V	6
Zayin	weapon	Z	7
Cheth	fence	long E/Ch	8
Teth	snake	Th/T	9
Yod	hand	I	10
Caph	palm of the hand	K	20
Lamed	ox-goad	L	30
Mem	water	M	40
Nun	fish	N	50
Samech	support	hard Ch/S	60
Ayin	eye	O	70
Peh	mouth	P	80
Tzadi	fish hook	Q/Tz	90
Qoph	back of head	R/Rh/Q	100
Resh	head	S/R	200
Shin	tooth	T/Sh	300
Tav	cross	Y/U/Th	400
Caph (final)		Ph	500
Mem (final)		Ch	600
Nun (final)		Ps	700
Peh (final)		long O	800
Tzadi (final)		S	900

Figure 5-24 Hebrew Gematria Chart

Ferocious "king of the jungle"? Sure, but the added meanings are more likely to give us true guides for *human* action and understanding as we traverse the jungle of modern life.

True gematria practitioners would explore not only the lion's metaphoric complexity, but seek out his numeric counterparts as well: What other words total 160? How might they join with our lion to further enhance our understanding?

The Babylonians also had a gematria system. King Sargon II (flourished 720 BCE) had a wall constructed to the length of 16,283 cubits, based on the numerical value of his name.[16] This grandiose example can be an inspiration for our own practical uses of gematria, not for massive walls, perhaps, but for more modest forms of measurement and counting, based on the gematria value of a proper name or a quality we wish to invoke. So if I were making a talisman to invoke those lionlike qualities mentioned previously, maybe I'd decorate it with 160 beads.

The Greek letters have their own numerical values, and their own tradition of study. For example, the Gnostic deity Abraxas has the numerical value of 365 (1 + 2 + 100 + 1 + 60 + 1 + 200), equal to the number of days in the year.[17]

In traditional practice, scholars apply gematria to sacred texts, seeking words with equal numeric values. Once discovered, a scholar could follow these numerically resonant threads off into countless directions. The result? Secret harmonies hidden in an interconnected web of meaning, all invisible to a casual reader of the same text.

Bring patience: This can easily be the work of decades.

Letter	Name	Value
A α	Alpha	1
B β	Beta	2
Γ γ	Gamma	3
Δ δ	Delta	4
E ε	Epsilon	5
ς ϖ	Digamma	6
Z ζ	Zeta	7
H η	Eta	8
Θ θ	Theta	9
I ι	Iota	10
K κ	Kappa	20
Λ λ	Lambda	30
M μ	Mu	40
N ν	Nu	50
Ξ ξ	Xei	60
O o	Omicron	70
Π π	Pi	80
ϑ φ	Qoppa	90
P ρ	Rho	100
Σ σ	Sigma	200
T τ	Tau	300
Y υ	Ypsilon	400
Φ φ	Phi	500
X χ	Chi	600
Ψ ψ	Psi	700
Ω ω	Omega	800

Figure 5-25 Greek Gematria Chart

Whether you used the chart in *Figure 5-20* or the one in *Figure 5-22*, we're now ready to proceed. We're going to "write" the phrase "Run well Be safe" into the Mars square *(Figure 5-15)* using the numbers we just worked out. At this point, tracing paper, ruler, and eraser will be handy. "Test-drive" your phrase first on tracing paper laid over the magical square. That way, you can familiarize yourself with where your numbers are and prevent nasty mistakes on a hand-drawn square you've labored long to create. See *Figure 5-26* for an example of how to get started. You can also make sure your phrase yields a pleasing design rather than a deranged-looking snarl. Edit and reword if you like—that's what tracing paper and erasers are for. Draw the lines freehand, or use the ruler if you want them super-straight. Once you're sure where you're going, remove the tracing paper, and with focused intentions inscribe your lines on to the square itself.

Figure 5-26 Mars start of phrase: Here are the first four "letters" (R-u-n w) symbolized by numbers 18 (with a star), 21, 14, and 23. Nothing too tough, but remember, short phrases work better than wordy epics. *Figure 5-27* depicts how the finished product should look.

Figure 5-27. Mars end of phrase. The finished product, with a coherent overall shape, marked with a white star at the other end.

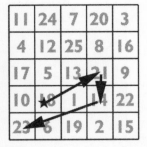

Figure 5-26 Mars start of phrase

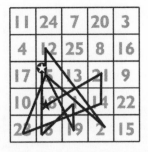

Figure 5-27 Mars end of phrase

Traditionally these squares are created when the chosen planet is overhead in the sky and well aspected astrologically to other planets. You may prefer to simply work on the day associated with that planet. If you like, cast a circle and call the directions before you begin.

Experiment all you like with different colors and types of markers and colored pencils, exotic papers, or whatever strikes your fancy. Once you have your line pattern, it can also be carved or embroidered, scratched in the dirt, traced upon the surface of your bathwater or above ceremonial libations. The possibilities are endless. Keep notes on how you use the squares. These notes become your reference or recipe book for future use. If something works especially well, you can repeat it, and if something doesn't seem to work, you can make necessary changes.

Other Things to Do with Magical Squares

- Find the "magical line" in each square. Do this by starting at number 1, drawing a line to number 2, then to number 3, and onward in numerical order through the square to its final number. You'll find great geometric patterns that may have other design possibilities for you. Garden layout? Business logo? Tattoo? Overlaid on the map of your choice as a vacation route?
- Trace your birth date and time on to a square as a way to invoke all the positive talents and potential you brought with you to this life. Use the square for the planet that rules your sun sign, or for the planet whose position you find most challenging in your chart, or do this with every square and then compare. You may find a line design you can develop into a truly personal magical symbol.

Luna's Labyrinth

Searching for ever-more square magic, I turned to Clifford A. Pickover's wonderful *The Zen of Magic Squares, Circles, and Stars*. Using an order-9 magic square (*not* the Square of the Moon), Pickover found a pleasing geometric pattern by blacking out all the odd numbers.[18] I copied his idea using tracing paper over the same-size order-9 square, the real Square of the Moon (*Figure 5-19*). Because I used a different square, I found a totally different pattern. With a shock of recognition, I realized I was looking at the "seed diagram" for a seven-circuit labyrinth, as shown in *Figures 5-28 and 29*.

Versions of this labyrinth are found worldwide, from ancient Crete to the American Southwest and everywhere in between. I learned the "seed diagram"—the basis for drawing the design—in a labyrinth workshop, creating a large one on the sandy shore of a mountain lake.[19] An upright + (plus sign) in the middle, four angled L-shapes, and four corner dots are all it takes. These components are hidden in plain sight in the Square of the Moon, visible once all the odd numbers are blacked out.

Allowing plenty of space to all sides, scratch the seed diagram large into beach sand or draw it small on a sheet of paper, and then begin. After connecting the top of the main vertical line to the top of the upper-right L (as shown in *Figure 5-29*), continue working around in left-to-right arcs (*Figures 5-30 and 5-31*). Generally, if you start from a line, you'll land on a dot, and vice versa. Note that the U-turn "corners" where you loop back in the labyrinth are also the outer corners of the Square of the Moon.

Rather like the Moon herself, waxing and waning left to right while moving across the sky left to right, you must move both *deosil* and *widdershins* while within the labyrinth. Making one large enough to walk is wonderful—creative lawn-mowing?—but you can also create a far more portable finger–size version. Try coloring one with a spectrum–range of colored pencils, blending from one color to the next as you round the corners.

Several odd additional notes:

First: The Square of the Moon has 81 cells and numbers, and the Moon itself is $\frac{1}{81}$ of Earth's mass.[20]

Next: The Earth is moving through space at 28 miles per hour; the Moon at 2,268 miles per hour. That means the Moon is going 81 times as fast as the Earth.[21]

Finally: A Mayan carving in Palenque states, "81 moons make 2,392 days."[22] Divide 2,392 by 81 and you get 29.53, equal to modern science's reckoning of days per Moon cycle.

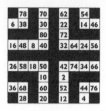

Figure 5-28 Square of the moon showing labyrinth "seed' pattern along odd-numbered lines

Figure 5-29 Labyrinth with first arc drawn

Figure 5-30 Labyrinth with second and third arcs

Figure 5-31 Labyrinth with fourth and fifth arcs added

Figure 5-32 Labyrinth with arcs 6, 7, and 8 added, we now have
a completed 7-circuit labyrinth

History and Speculative Lore of the Templars

Circa 42: Mary Magdalen arrives on the southern coast of France. She's accompanied by her relatives and friends, and she's pregnant or has a young child with her.

The 300s–400s: The Merovingian line of secular rulers officially began with Mérovée (circa 374–circa 425). The misty lore around Mérovée claims he was the son of both King Clodio and of a fantastic sea creature that his pregnant mother encountered while swimming. Tracing farther back, one of Mérovée's ancestors was fabled to be Mary Magdalen. Perhaps Mérovée's fabled sea creature is a metaphoric link to the seafaring Mary Magdalen, a means of declaring that his bloodline came from the sea.[2] Weirdly, Mérovée's son, King Childeric I, was buried with both a crystal ball and a severed horse's head, an odd echo of our chessboard Knight.[3]

The 600s: A descendant of Mérovée, Dagobert II (651–679) was carried into hiding in Ireland after his father's death in 656. Raised in the monastery at Slane, he married a Celtic princess and was eventually able to return to France. Widowed, Dagobert wed for a second time, to Giselle de Razès, the niece of the Visigoth king. The wedding took place at her home in the village of Rennes-de-Chateau. Their son Sigebert was born in 676, around the time Dagobert successfully established himself on the throne of Austrasia, in the north of what is now France. But on December 23, 679, while resting midhunt in the Forest of Woëvre, Dagobert II was murdered, stabbed through the eye.[4] Allegedly, young Sigebert and his mother fled south to her home city of Rennes-de-Château where the boy became Duke of Razès and Count of the Rhedae (an early name for Rennes-de-Château). Whatever Sigebert's later fate, the Mérovée bloodline continued in his Celtic half-sisters and others in the Merovingian line; one of Charlemagne's wives is said to have been a Merovingian princess.[5]

The 1000s: When Jerusalem fell in the First Crusade, French Knight Godefroy de Bouillon was chosen on July 22, 1099 (feast day of Mary Magdalen), to rule the region. Some accounts trace Godefroy's lineage to the Merovingians and view his role in Jerusalem as a hereditary retaking of the city, just as some versions of this tale credit Godefroy with founding the Priory of Sion to guard the secret of his Merovingian bloodline.

The 1100s: According to their own early historian, Guillaume de Tyre, the Order of the Poor Knights of the Temple of Solomon—the Knights Templar—were founded in 1118, under the auspices of Baudouin I, King of Jerusalem, brother of the late Godefroy. These first knights took their name from the location of their living quarters, atop the ancient site of King Solomon's Temple. Their order was both monastic and military, vowed to obedience, piety, poverty, and chastity, and initially devoted to the protection of pilgrims. By 1139, their ranks had swelled and their power was such that Pope Innocent II declared that the Templars owed no allegiance to any temporal authority—church or ruler—other than himself and subsequent popes.[6] Bertrand de Blanchefort was the fourth Grand Master of the Knights Templar, from 1156 until his death. The Blancheforts had deep roots in the Razès /Rennes-de-Château area.

This was an era of great cathedral construction. The Templars are strongly associated now with the Merovingian bloodline, safeguarding it and the proofs that Jesus and Mary Magdalen were married and had children, but the Templars (and their wealth) are also credited with a role in building many of the great Gothic cathedrals. The term gothic purportedly comes not from the Goths or Visigoths, but from the Greek word goetic, meaning "magical action." By some accounts, Templar stonemasons—trained by Eastern mathematicians?—brought sacred geometry into their designs and methods of construction,[7] and these highly skilled craftsmen would surely have been in the early guilds of master masons, teaching—and guarding—the secrets of their craft, as the Freemasons, both "operative" and "speculative," do today.

Many Gothic churches are dedicated to Notre-Dame, presumed to mean the Virgin Mary. But Notre-Dame simply means "Our Lady" or "Our Queen." This would be an excellent way to hide something in plain sight: the veneration of Mary Magdalen as the wife of Jesus, spiritual queen and Great Mother of France's once and future kings. These churches often were built atop earlier goddess temples, and many originally had statues of their dame either hidden in crypts or portrayed as dark-complected "Black Virgins."

There's a further connection to a woman who is "dark," or unseen, in this case because she occupies the night sky as Virgo, the zodiac's sole feminine star group. Many of France's great Notre-Dame cathedrals appear to be laid out across the land in the pattern of this constellation. Louis Charpentier introduced this idea in his 1975 book *The Mysteries of Chartres Cathedral*.[8]

This might sound like just another Templar-related "Elvis-sighting" if Charpentier's maps didn't look so intriguing. My version of this theory appears in *Figure 6-4*, with star-and-cathedral pairings slightly different from those Charpentier found. Modern graphics allowed a map of northern France to be marked with Notre-Dame sites, then replaced with vintage Virgo art circa 1825. Both map and virgin were rotated and resized to align

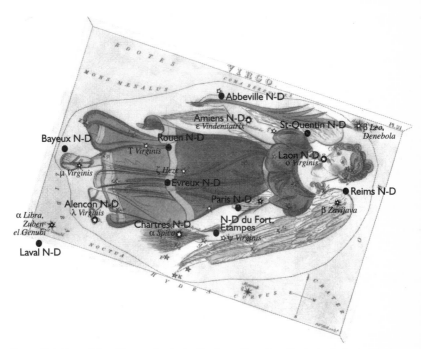

Figure 6-4 Map of the Virgo cathedrals. Northern French cathedrals dedicated to "Our Lady" overlaid on the constellation Virgo. White stars and italics represent stars; black dots represent Notre-Dame cathedrals ("N-D").

them, but not "stretched" or skewed out of their original shapes. Granted, with enough shrink-and-tilt action, any two sites can be made to match up in this manner, but here we see four exact alignments—marked with white stars inside the black "cathedral" dots—and several others darn close. Chartres, Amiens, Alencon, and Laon all pair precisely with stars in the Virgo group; Abbeville and Etampes both come pretty close, with other sites less convincingly placed.

Perhaps significantly, Amiens—France's largest Gothic cathedral—was built specifically to house the head of John the Baptist, whose saint day on June 24 is special to Freemasons.[9] Two of the greatest Notre-Dame cathedrals, at Chartres and Amiens, align with Virgo's key stars, Spica ("the spike of grain") and Vindemiatrix ("the grape-gatherer.")

Consider that Virgo and Pisces are opposite each other in the zodiac, and we find good alchemical fusion-of-opposites imagery: Mary Magdalen as the Virgo grain-mother faces Jesus the Piscean fisher-of-men. They balance each other as Virgo and Pisces across the heavens. Miracles of loaves and fishes, indeed.

The 1200s: Inspired by a secret gospel of St. John called the "Gospel of Love," the Cathars were followers of Christ, but believed that Jesus was human rather than divine, putting them at odds with the Church of Rome. Their priesthood was open to both men and women, who practiced herbalism, vegetarianism, celibacy, tolerance, simplicity, and pacifism. Cathar laypeople followed the messages of simplicity and tolerance, but weren't under the strictures that forbade meat, marriage, and sex.

What sounds like a small band of happy hippies was a widespread and very populous group that attracted followers from all levels of society. In the Languedoc region of southern France, there were Cathar dioceses in Agen, Albi, Carcassonne, Toulouse, and Razès, as well as two dioceses elsewhere, in Champagne in the north and another ministering to France at large. Another twelve Cathar dioceses existed throughout Italy, Lombardy, Tuscany, and the Balkans.[10] These same regions often had Black Virgin statues and/or churches dedicated to Mary Magdalen.[11] Committed to universal literacy and the belief that the gospel should be available in each local language, Cathars were prominent in the paper industry, and—via literacy and their egalitarian view of women—were an active influence on the flowering of arts and letters throughout the Languedoc.[12]

As the Cathars grew internationally, the Church of Rome reacted. In 1209, Pope Innocent III declared religious war: the Albigensian Crusade, named for the Cathar center at Albi. Innocent III's recruiting bonus was a fiendishly generous deal: absolution of all past sins and any new sins committed while fighting. Under papal license, these "crusaders" could seize the property of anyone they deemed a heretic and do whatever they deemed necessary in defense of the church. Ambitious and ruthless warriors from every level of society signed up, and clergymen went along to conduct heresy trials. Although Innocent III called this a "crusade" (making the absolutions and papal licenses official), notably both the Knights Templar and the Order of the Knights Hospitaller avoided active involvement.[13]

The attack began at Béziers in July 1209. The Cathars had peacefully coexisted with the city's Jews and predominant Catholics. The Jews, who had been subjected to this sort of insidious targeting before, wisely fled. The "crusaders" killed everyone who remained, slaughtering an estimated 20,000. Béziers fell on July 22, the feast day of Mary Magdalen. The Albigensian Crusade's indiscriminate brutality and heretic burnings spread throughout the Languedoc. Rennes-la-Château fell in 1210, and its fortifications were pulled down.

The Cathars, numerous and with family ties to the Templars and the region's aristocracy, held out for years. Montségur, their final stronghold, surrendered in 1244 after a yearlong siege. According to lore, some Cathars managed to escape at the end, not to save themselves, but to preserve a treasure that was never identified.

Throughout the Albigensian Crusade, the Templars quietly aided escaping Cathars, with whom they often shared family ties. The two groups are believed to have shared something else: the belief—or knowledge—that Jesus was married to Mary Magdalen.

The 1300s: The Knights Templar themselves were put down, brutally and conclusively. They had grown wealthy and powerful beyond the scope of church and state, whether through their financial acumen or through knowledge they held and perhaps intended to use. The insolvent King Philippe IV of France and the pope he had helped bring to power, Clement V, moved to break the Templar strength. Carefully coordinated attacks were conducted throughout France on October 13, 1307, and Templars were captured, tortured, and executed all through the land.

By some accounts, a small group of Templars at Bézu, near Rennes-la-Château, weren't targeted, perhaps because of ancestral ties to families there. Pope Clement V was himself the son of Ida de Blanchefort, a descendant of Bertrand de Blanchefort, former Templar Grand Master.[14] Again, rumors persist that some Templars escaped with an unnamed treasure.

The 1700s: Marie, Marquise d'Hautpoul de Blanchefort, nee Marie de Nègre d'Arles, died on January 17, 1781. Abbé Bigou—chaplain to the d'Hautpoul/de Blanchfort families, parish priest of Rennes-le-Château, and Marie's confessor—is said to have labored for two years afterward over the precise text to be placed on her stele-and-slab grave marker in his church's cemetery. France was already in the throes of social unrest that in 1788 became the French Revolution. Abbé Bigou saw the strange inscription carved, then escaped into Spain.

We turn now to more recent times and Rennes-le-Château, the small town in the south of France. The modest village church is still dedicated to Mary Magdalene, as it has been since ancient times.

In 1885, a new parish priest named Bérenger Saunière arrived to take charge of the church. His official annual pay was only about six Euros, and he hunted and fished to supplement his larder. Saunière befriended a neighboring priest in Renne-les-Bains, the Abbé Boudet, and in other ways settled into his parish. But Saunière's *manner* of settling in is what continues to spark interest in Rennes-le-Château and Bérenger Saunière.

Soon after Saunière's arrival, he had the church's altar replaced. One of the twin pillars from the old stone Visigoth-era altar purportedly contained parchments written in code, which Saunière devoted himself to translating.

Within a few years, a spate of pricey "upgrades" began. New stained glass windows. A statue of the Virgin, incongruously wearing the "castle-crown" of St. Barbara, patroness of architects and stonemasons. A new holy water font, held up by a garishly painted demon. Saunière bought land throughout the area, registering the deeds in the name of Marie Dénarnaud, his housekeeper. He built a luxurious mansion, Villa Bethania; a green house; a library tower, Tour Magdala; he bought statues, bas-reliefs, a new pulpit, Stations of the Cross, and a baptismal font; under his direction gardeners created orangeries and promenades.

Where did Saunière get the cash for all this flash?

The main theories seem to be magic, murder, blackmail, and buried treasure.

Magic: Did a giant natural pentacle in the Rennes-le-Château landscape assist in Saunière's performance of the "Convocation of Venus" spell, granting him the power of accurate occult predictions on behalf of very generous clients?

Murder: A notary was shot to death right after Saunière helped him translate an old will in Latin. What provoked the accident, which occurred in Saunière's presence? Who hacked to death the reclusive priest in nearby Coustaussa on the eve of All Saints' Day, 1897—Samhain? His papers were rifled and perhaps stolen, his body arranged as if lying in state, and there was no sign of forced entry, no hand or footprints left behind.

Blackmail: Did Saunière discover a Priory of Sion/Templar/Cathar secret and get either the elusive "PS," the Vatican, or someone else to pay for his silence?

Buried treasure: Did Saunière find (choose at least one) the treasure of Merovingian King Dagobert II? Jewish Holy Land treasure—including the Ark of the Covenant—brought to Rome by Titus, then looted away by the Visigoths? Cathar treasure secretly carried away when Montségur fell in 1244? Treasure stashed around nearby Templar strongholds at Château Blanchefort or Bézu? Wealth-generating secrets left behind by early alchemists or Rosicrucians? Riches hidden during the French Revolution by optimistic aristocrats who lost their heads and never returned?

Mayhem, greed, knights, hidden treasure, suspicions, murder . . . shades of *The Maltese Falcon.* Where's Sam Spade when we need him, murmuring about "the stuff that dreams are made of" as he bids farewell to the iconic black bird?

Instead we return to our chessboard, and remove all the players except for a single Knight. We work from a text taken from the upright stele on the grave of Marie, the text Abbé Bigou labored so to compose. His inscription goes like this:

CT GIT NOBLe M	(line 1)
ARIE DE NEGRe	(line 2)
DABLES DAME	(line 3)
DHAUPOUL De	(line 4)
BLANCHEFORT	(line 5)
AGEE DE SOIX	(line 6)
ANTE SEpTaNS	(line 7)
DECEDEE LE	(line 8)
XVII JANVIER	(line 9)
MCCOLXXXXI	(line 10)
REQUIES CATIN	(line 11)
PACE	(line 12)
(P.S.) PRAE-CUM	(line 13)

Bigou's very peculiar misspellings are believed to be intentional, part of a code. Why else split up the letters of "M-arie," and misspell both "Arles" and "Hautpoul"? Certainly you'd want to spell your patroness's name correctly, unless you had a darn good reason not to. And what priest could misspell "requiescat in pace"? Bigou's erroneous break in the lettering of this standard Latin phrase creates catin, which has several meanings. And that "(P.S.)" at the end is a red flag for Priory of Sion buffs.

We begin by collecting the mistakes. In upper case letters, that's the T in "CT" (which should be "CI") and the dangling M from "Marie" at the end of the first line. We get B from "DABLES" in line 3—it ought to read "D'AR-LES." Down in line 10, we find an O where the Roman numerals need a third C for 1781. In lower case letters, we collect an e in lines 1, 2, and 4, and finally a p in line 7. From this odd selection, scholars of the Templar-mysteries spell *MORT épée,* which most literally means "death sword." With these eight letters removed, 128 remain. That's double the number of cells on a chessboard.

Now we come to the very bizarre decoding process, for apparently this is what Abbé Bigou worked so long to design. The code is keyed to 128 specific letters in one of the parchments discovered by Bérenger Saunière. The cipher is worked using a 1-to-25 letter chart (no W in French). Slowly, the value of each parchment code-letter is added to the value of a letter from the "MORT épée" phrase, then to the value of a letter from the complete misspelled phrase on Marie's grave, rendered into numbers and *written backwards*. The alleged result is an alphabet-soup of 128 new leters, which are written onto two chessboards, top to bottom, *left to right* on the first board, and top to bottom, *left to right* on the second.

And now, finally we return to our theme, the Knight's Tour. The Knight is put through his paces, first on one board, and then—identically, but as if seen in a horizontal reflection—on the other board, spelling out new words by the order in which each move occurs.[15] *(Figure 6-5.)*

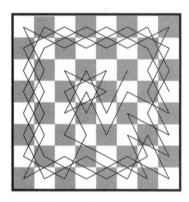

Figure 6-5 Knight's tour of the encoded phrase

Here is what emerges:
BERGERE PAS DE TENTATION QUE POUSSIN
TENIERS GARDENT LE CLEF PAX DCLXXXI PAR LA
CROIX ET CE CHEVAL DE DIEU J'ACHEVE CE
DAEMON DE GARDIEN A MIDI POMMES BLEUES

In English, this is purported to read:

SHEPHERDESS NO TEMPTATION TO WHICH POUSSIN AND TENIERS KEEP THE KEY PEACE 681 WITH THE CROSS AND THIS HORSE OF GOD I REACH THIS DAEMON GUARDIAN AT MIDDAY BLUE APPLES

Abbé Bigou was well placed to protect Marie's family secrets, whether they involved monetary inheritances or secret secular/spiritual genealogies. He heard her final confession, he slowly arranged for the carvings on her gravestones, and, as parish priest in the Church of St. Mary Magdalen, he could easily have hidden the parchments that Saunière found years later during the altar's renovation. And he certainly had no reason to make anything easy for whoever found his clues.

But even when deciphered, this text still seems decidedly odd, so let's look more closely at all of the words, translated, decoded, and otherwise.

Start with *catin* in line 11 on the stele. It's French slang for "prostitute," but also means "cavity" or "cave" in the local dialect. Unless Bigou is calling his patroness Marie a whore, this seems like both a reference to alleged prostitute Mary Magdalen and a clue to a hiding place.[16]

Nicolas Poussin (1594–1665) and the two David Teniers ("the Elder," 1598–1649, and his son "the Younger," 1610–1690) are painters strongly linked to Rennes-le-Château lore, particularly Poussin's *Les Bergers d'Arcadie (The Shepherds of Arcadia)*. In fact, another of the chaplain's coded phrases, on the horizontal slab of Marie's grave in a weird jumble of Latin and Greek letters and Templar crosses, is rendered *Et in Arcadia Ego* ("And in Arcadia I am"). That's the same phrase Poussin's shepherds and shepherdess find on the tomb in his painting. *Arcadia* can refer metaphorically to any place of pastoral simplicity, but a nearby town named Arques offers other possibilities. Arques is thought to be the painting's setting, and it sits on the old Rose Line, the French 0° longitude line that runs through the Church of Saint-Sulpice in Paris.

That odd phrase "death sword" is open to other readings, too. *Mort* is indeed "death," but also can mean "lifeless," or just "stagnant." As for "sword," besides the fatal blade that pierced Dagobert II's eye, let's consider that the *fleur-de-lys*, the iris, was the royal emblem of the Merovingians. The iris's Latin name is *gladiolus*, which means "small sword," in token of its bladelike leaves.[17] With Dagobert II's demise, the Merovingian *fleur-de-lys* line became stagnant, or at least uncertain.

Can anyone study this material without forming her own wild theories? I succumbed, and my preferred expanded reading of the translation is this:

> Marie, in your role as shepherdess-guardian, no temptations appear when Poussin and Teniers guard the key to your secret's peace, since the Woman here is not Eve-the-tempress. Remember 681 [when Dagobert II's son Sigebert was brought to Rennes-le-Château]. With the help of God and this chessboard Knight-horse, I craft this code to be as a guardian-spirit: Seek in the Midi among the grapes.

"Midday" is a fine translation, and perhaps that's when the Sun is at the correct angle for a site to be found. High noon should put the light and shadows on a direct north-south line, and in fact the "Rose Line" also passes through the neighboring village of Rennes-des-Bains. But the region is itself called the Midi, in addition to its other names, old and new: Lanquedoc, Occitania, Septimania ("SEpT"?), modern Provence.

Those "blue apples" can be grapes planted or carved near the hiding place, identified in this way as a contrast to Eve's tempting red apple, just as the Virgin Mary might be thought of as the White Queen, and Mary Magdalen as the Black Queen, the hidden queen. Not good versus bad, but visible versus hidden.

Tempting, blue or otherwise, we should pay special heed to these apples because, unlike any other Knight's Tours I could find, Abbé Bigou's route creates a five-pointed star as it moves between its first eight cells. *(Figure 6-6.)* It looks like Abbé Bigou intentionally placed a reference to the divine feminine, and her hidden seedlings, right in the middle of his chessboard.

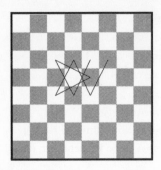

Figure 6-6 The hidden star at the beginning

We find a seed-laden star within each apple we cut horizontally, and the tree is sacred to Venus, whose planet draws a pentagram in its orbit over the course of eight years, returning then to its starting point, like a *reentrant* Knight's Tour. The Knights Templars were aware of Venus' orbital star *(see Chapter 10);* we'll look more closely at the planet and her pentagram later.

While grapes don't have such an obvious association to the star shape, they do have a subtle built-in connection to the number 5. Where the stem meets the leaf, each grape-leaf branches into five clearly visible veins, like a wrist and hand branching into five fingers.

Grapes are significant. In addition to their broad planetary associations to Venus via Dionysus, they can refer very specifically to the Mary Magdalen-Jesus genealogy, symbolically portrayed as a vine. This is traditional genealogy lingo, for example: "Thy wife is like a fruitful vine" (Psalms 28), or "Your mother is like a vine planted by the water, fruitful and branchy . . . but she was torn up . . . and now she is planted in the desert . . . She is now without a royal branch, a ruler's specter" (Ezekiel 19:10-14). The Bible contains many other passages using the vine as lineage-metaphor for the chosen people of God. Although the biblical references predate the Merovingians, the metaphor continued to be used, and Merovingian descendants referred to themselves as the "Vine."[18] And among the papermaking Cathars, the image of twin pillars supporting grapes was a distinguishing watermark.[19] And remember Virgo's star, Vindemiatrix, is "the grape-gatherer."

If you travel to Rennes-le-Château, don't bother looking for Marie's grave. The details are known now only because a science group had made records as a local curiosity. To the dismay of his parishioners, Bérenger Saunière destroyed the marquise's gravestones.

Amid the speculative conclusions, some numbers are factual, visibly placed in the landscape. To honor Mary Magdalen and her July 22 feast day,

Saunière repeated the number 22 throughout his garish alterations: Twenty-two steps going up in his tower, twenty-two steps going down within his greenhouse, two terraces of eleven steps each into the garden, and other expressions of 22. And, maybe as a nod to a Knight's Tour that helped pay for it all, Saunière had one floor tiled in an 8-by-8 grid.[20]

And in the end, there were more numbers. After a visit by "mysterious strangers," Bérenger Saunière suffered a heart attack on January 17, 1917. That's the date on which Marie, Marquise d'Hautpoul de Blanchefort, died in 1781, 136 years earlier.

Saunière died a few days later, on the 22nd, of course.

CHAPTER 7

Shapes and Numbers
Meditation

Maybe due to years in the visual arts, I find I prefer at times to work with the numbers as shapes, making each one visual. This short meditation has helped expand my understanding of the first four numbers and given me a far clearer sense of how each can be used symbolically.

Meditation Instructions

The basic instructions are bare-bones and simple. The discussion of symbolism later in the chapter can help enrich the instructions. Read through all this to get the general idea (or have a friend read it aloud for you, or make an audiotape), then close your eyes.

1. In your mind's eye, see a straight, flat line. Breathe deeply as you look at this wide, open horizon. *(Figure 7-1.)*

2. Now curve this line until its ends meet and you have a circle. *(Figure 7-2.)*

3. Breathe with this circle a while, then gradually fold it down into itself to create the shape of the Crescent Moon, its two points aiming upward like a bowl. *(Figure 7-3.)*

4. Now, as you continue breathing deeply, let this curving bowl reshape itself, straightening and extending upward until it has three lines, in an upward-pointing triangle.

5. Breathe deeply and let the shape change again, opening out at the top to add a fourth line, taking the shape of a square, very calm, very stable.

6. Breathe with this square shape and then let it shift again, narrowing at the bottom and changing into a downward-pointing triangle.

7. Breathe with this triangle and then watch it shift again, softening and curving its lines into the shape of a valentine heart.

8. Breathe with this heart and then let its two corners soften and disappear until the heart becomes a circle.

9. Breathe with this circle, then let it open, becoming a straight vertical line between Earth and Sky.

The Symbolism of the Meditation

The first line *(Figure 7-1)* is the horizon. In a landscape painting, we see just this short horizontal line, but in real life, that horizon line is a great circle and we stand at its center. This is our earthly reality, as the horizon encircles us.

The circle *(Figure 7-2)* is also a symbol for Air and the East, and the dawn Sun. The circle is a closed shape that can be drawn with one line. If you want to animate this image to make it more vivid, try picturing Ouroborus, the great snake holding its own tail in its mouth, a living-circle symbol of continuity.

Figure 7-1 Horizontal line

Figure 7-2 Circle

The crescent *(Figure 7-3)* is a symbol for Water and the West, and for the new Crescent Moon, first seen in the West at sunset. The crescent is drawn with two lines. Animate this shape as that young Crescent Moon against the darkening night sky, or see it as your own hands, cupped, holding moonlit water.

The up-pointing triangle *(Figure 7-4)* symbolizes Fire, the South, and male energies. The triangle is drawn with three lines. This can also be pictured as one of the pyramids, or as an active, leaping flame.

Figure 7-3 Crescent Moon

Figure 7-4 Triangle pointing up

The square *(Figure 7-5)* is a symbol for the North and the element of Earth, and it's drawn with four lines. It can be a house, a table, an altar, a child's building block, one cube from a pair of dice.

The down-pointing triangle *(Figure 7-6)* is a symbol of female energies, and again is drawn with three lines. Animate this image as a spinning top, or as a funnel cloud.

Figure 7-5 Square

Figure 7-6 Triangle pointing down

Then let either of these whirling shapes shift to become a living, beating heart *(Figure 7-7.)* The curved lines mirror each other, symbolizing connection, love, and compassion. Like the crescent—the hands cupping water—the heart contains and nourishes, and is drawn with two lines.

Figure 7-7 Heart

Figure 7-8 Circle at end pointing up

Figure 7-9 Vertical line

We return again to the circle *(Figure 7-8)*, as the circle of All Creation, unity and wholeness, again drawn with a single line. See yourself encircled by the landscape, standing tall within the living circle of the horizon in the terrain of your choice.

The vertical line *(Figure 7-9)* represents the connection between Earth and Sky, between us, on our earthly plane, and the Higher Powers, however we choose to define them. At the center of the horizon-circle, stand upright with arms stretched overhead. Feel yourself as a conduit of the energies between the Earth and the heavens. With several deep breaths, bring all the energy you need back into yourself and open your eyes.

This is a meditation of numbers and elements and imagination. If your own imagination is piqued by it, work with the exercise further by finding simple objects to express each shape. It's likely to be an odd assortment. Good! Unlikely juxtapositions shake us out of routine expectations.

As a struggling artist in the 1950s, Robert Rauschenberg found his materials on the streets of New York City. His "Combine" painting-and-assemblage creations presented the "found objects"—a.k.a. cast-off junk—in startling new contexts.

If your environment isn't as urban-trash-diverse as New York City, look to the earth art of Andy Goldsworthy. His creations are elegant, temporary, and assembled in Nature, using only what he finds there. Fallen leaves, stones, dandelion heads, icicles—the materials are painstakingly arranged and photographed. Then they blow, float, decompose, or melt away.

Whether you gravitate toward the quirky results of Rauschenberg or the sublime results of Goldsworthy, give this technique a shot. The results may astonish you. Whatever you discover, use your assorted *objets d'art* as quiet reminders for this meditation.

KABBALAH AND THE TREE OF LIFE

Having just looked at very simple shapes that relate to numbers, let's look briefly at a more complex form.

We're sensate creatures living on such a relatively lush planet, not perfect—global warming, natural disasters, personal woes—but reasonably hospitable, and we can't seem to get away from finding natural world metaphors for our most spiritual endeavors. One of the most profound symbols is the Kabbalistic Tree of Life. Ten key positions—the *sephirah*—are connected and interconnected by twenty-two pathways. Simplified illustrations make its tree-form more apparent, and by just connecting the key-stations in numerical order, a lightning bolt can be found. *(Figure 7-10.)* Yes, lightning bolts in nature can destroy trees, but the point here can be more usefully seen as the dual images of energy blazing down from the heavens contrasted with life-force energy surging up from the Earth.

Studies using the Kabbalah and the Tree of Life date back to the sixth century, at least, and perhaps as early as the third century. One key text, *Zohar*, or *The Book of Splendor*, was written in the twelfth century by a Spanish rabbi, during a time when Jewish culture was flowering in that country and in nearby Provence.[1]

According to writer A. E. Waite (designer of the Rider-Waite-Smith Tarot deck), the word *Kabbalah* comes from a Hebrew root meaning "to receive," and its students can enhance their "reception" through its study.[2] The Kabbalah, like so many topics worth understanding, reveals itself gradually over time, so all we'll look at here are some basic signposts.

Each sephiroth has its own meaning, or layers of meanings. *(Figure 7-11.)*

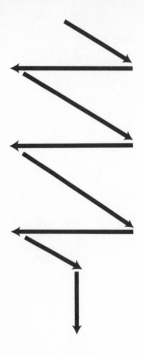

Figure 7-10 Lightning

Figure 7-11 Kabbalah Tree of Life

1. *Kefer is the Crown:* The Divine Source of All, flowing from world to spirit, and from spirit to world. The power of Will, before there is distinct thought. In the human body, Kefer corresponds to the head.

2. *Chokmah is Wisdom:* Also called Ab (Father), associated with the "male" principle, the "active potency" that sparks awareness. In the human body, Chokmah corresponds to the brain.

3. *Binah is Understanding:* Also called Ama (Mother), associated with the passive "feminine" principle. After the will and awareness of Kefer and Chokmah, Binah represents integration. In the human body, Binah corresponds to the heart. Its planetary connection is to Saturn.

4. *Chesed is Love:* Mercy, love, loving-kindness, and what is some
   times called caritas. Unbounded nurturing, healing, and compassion.
   In the human body, Chesed corresponds to the right arm. Its
   planetary connection is to Jupiter.

5. *Geburah is Strength:* Its themes include judgment, and possible
   severity. But more basically, it refers to the boundaries, definition,
   discipline and limitations of social order and identity. In the
   human body, Geburah corresponds to the left arm. Its planet-
   connection is Mars.

6. *Tiphareth is Beauty:* Compassion, order and universal harmony
   are the themes here. Giving and receiving, and the balance point
   of justice. In the human body, Tiphareth corresponds to the chest
   or torso. Its planetary connection is to the Sun.

7. *Netzach is Victory:* This is a place of warrior energy, confident
   force, and success. Sometimes perceived as "parent" energy. In
   the human body, Netzach corresponds to the right leg. Its
   planetary connection is to Venus.

8. *Hod is Glory:* Splendor is another name. Here we find vulnerability and dependence in contrast to Netzach. Sometimes
   perceived as "child" energy. In the human body, Hod
   corresponds to the left leg. Its planetary connection is to Mercury.

9. *Yesod is Foundation:* Stability and corporeal reality. The balance
   between Netzach and Hod of independence and dependence.
   Magical work and powerful invocation are among the themes
   here. In the human body, Yesod corresponds to the sexual
   organs. Its planetary connection is to the Moon.

10. *Malkuth is Kingdom:* Also called the *Shekinah*, male and female
    attributions combine here as physical manifestations. Malkuth is
    both Adonai He-Aretz (Lord of Earth) and Kallah (the Bride). In
    the human body, Malkuth corresponds to the entire body. Its
    connection is to all the universe.[3]

Connecting these positions to each other are the twenty-two pathways. These are associated with both the Hebrew alphabet, as seen in the first twenty-two letters of the Hebrew gematria chart *(Figure 7-12)* and the twenty-two cards of the Tarot's Major Arcana—Kabbalah Tarot Chart. *(Figure 7-13.)* Some Tarot systems also equate the ten sephirah with the Minor Arcana cards, Ace through 10. The sephirah are clearly illustrated on the Ten of Pentacles in the Rider-Waite-Smith deck, floating in their Tree of Life arrangement in the foreground of the scene. And a hint of them is present on the partially-visible pomegranate tapestry hanging behind the High Priestess, suspended between her two pillars marked *B* and *J*. Boaz is the left pillar in the Tree of Life, the one symbolizing Strength, while Jachin is the right-hand pillar, the one symbolizing Wisdom. The High Priestess herself can be identified with the central pillar.[4]

Hebrew Name	Basic Meaning	Letter	Number
Aleph	cattle	A	1
Beth	house	B	2
Gimel	camel	C/G	3
Daleth	door	D	4
Heh	window	E/H	5
Vav	doorknob or nail	St/V	6
Zayin	weapon	Z	7
Cheth	fence	long E/Ch	8
Teth	snake	Th/T	9
Yod	hand	I	10
Caph	palm of the hand	K	11
Lamed	ox-goad	L	12
Mem	water	M	13
Nun	fish	N	14
Samech	support	hard Ch/S	15
Ayin	eye	O	16
Peh	mouth	P	17
Tzadi	fish hook	Q/Tz	18
Qoph	back of head	R/Rh/Q	19
Resh	head	S/R	20
Shin	tooth	T/Sh	21
Tav	cross	Y/U/Th	22

Figure 7-12 Hebrew Alphabet Chart

For interpretation and contemplation, you would look at the particulars of each connection. The Empress, for example, is Major Arcana card number 3, and is associated with pathway number 14, which is the bridge between Chokmah/Wisdom (2) and Binah/Understanding (3). What new insights might this provide into the Empress's esoteric meanings? What additional understandings can the 2s and 3s among the Minor Arcana cards bring?

Don't try this when you want a rapid interpretation in a reading. This is material for long and leisurely Tarot meditations.

Path	Card #	Tarot Card
11	0	The Fool
12	1	The Magician
13	2	The High Priestess
14	3	The Empress
15	4	The Emperor
16	5	The Hierophant
17	6	The Lovers
18	7	The Chariot
19	8	Strength
20	9	The Hermit
21	10	Wheel of Fortune
22	11	Justice
23	12	The Hanged Man
24	13	Death
25	14	Temperance
26	15	The Devil
27	16	The Tower
28	17	The Star
29	18	The Moon
30	19	The Sun
31	20	Judgment
32	21	The World

Figure 7-13 Kabbalah-Tarot Chart

CHAPTER 8

Pythagoras

There have been hundreds of mathematicians whose work influenced other mathematicians, but when we look for one who has also had a profound influence on metaphysical thought, we inevitably focus on Pythagoras.

Born on Samos, a Greek island, around 572 BCE, he's believed to have traveled widely—Egypt, perhaps India, and even Britain—before putting down roots in Crotona in southern Italy around 535 BCE.[1,2] In Crotona, a largely Greek settlement in Italy's "boot heel," Pythagoras thought, taught, and came to be venerated.

Was he himself truly taught by the Dactyls? These five magical beings were created by the Great Goddess Rhea, and their name—*Dactyl*—literally means "finger," or "digit."[3] Finger-counting was just one of the mysteries known to Pythagoras' student-disciples, the Pythagoreans.[4] Music and harmony, number symbolism, geometry, and all manner of mathematics were among their studies, which were closely held as secret teachings.

Some Pythagorean math can be expressed through groups of dots. The square groups shown here as *Figure 8-1* contain 1 (as a "seed"), 4, 9, 16, and 25 dots. In each case, these quantities are indeed squares of however many dots are in that square's row: The nine-dot square is built off a row of three, and 3 squared—3^2, or 3 x 3—equals 9.

As triangular groups we have 1 dot (as a "seed"), 3, 6, 10, and then 15, 21, and so on. *(Figure 8-2.)* The Pythagoreans held the ten-dot triangle in particular reverence and called it the "Holy Tetraktys," *tetra* referring to both its four-dot base and its internal math: 1 (uniqueness) + 2 (polarity) + 3 (harmony) + 4 (space and matter, and the four elements) = 10. Writing around 400 BCE, Pythagorean disciple Philolaus called the number 10 "sublime, potent and all-creating, the beginning and the guide of divine concerning life on Earth." The Tetraktys' three corner-dots guard a hexagon—6, symbolizing life—and the hexagon in turn encloses a lone dot known as "Athene," the same name as the ancient goddess of wisdom. *(Figure 8-3.)* To the Pythagoreans, this dot-Athene symbolized health, light, and intelligence.[5]

Let's look at just a bit more of Pythagoras' teaching via the Pythagorean triangle. This particular shape, shown in *Figure 8-4*, was valued as a high expression of order and harmony. It contains *one* right angle; *two* acute angles; sides measuring *three*, *four*, and *five* units in length along its edges; and its interior area equals *six* square units. Each of these numbers, 1 through 6, had its own larger, symbolic meanings.

Figure 8-1 Dots as squares

Figure 8-2 Dots as triangles

1 The "seed" again. Though the Pythagoreans didn't considered 1 to be a number, they saw it as the generator of all numbers.

2 This first female number was symbolic of opinion and the ability to divide.

3 The first male number was representative of harmony through the combination of 1 and 2.

4 This number represented justice and the four directions and was the basis for each edge of the Tetraktys.

5 Combining female and male, 2 and 3 symbolize love and union, both in human terms and in philosophical terms of synthesis.

6 The triangle's area of six squares expresses the first "perfect" number.

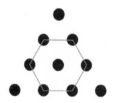

Figure 8-3 Tetraktys with hexagon surrounding the "Athene" central dot

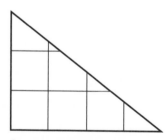

One right angle (90°)
Two acute angles (less than 90°)
Three squares in length along shortest side
Four squares in length along medium edge
Five squares in length along longest side
Six squares in total area

Figure 8-4 Pythagorean triangle

Perfect numbers are those equal to the sum of all the smaller numbers that divide into them—1 + 2 + 3 = 6—and we see that 6 can be multiplied to and evenly divided by those same numbers: 1 x 2 x 3 = 6, and 6 ÷ 3=2.

Getting back to the 3-4-5-sided Pythagorean triangle, there's a quick way to comprehend that it contains six squares. Trim down an index card so it measures 3-by-4 inches and mark it off into twelve 1-inch squares. Then cut it in half diagonally, as represented in *Figure 8-5*. Take a good look

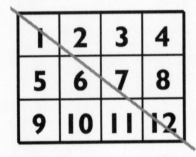

Figure 8-5 Cutting a numbered 3-by-4 rectangle to create a Pythagorean triangle

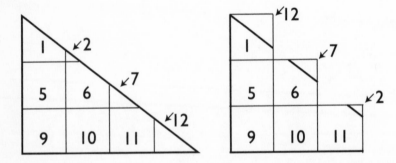

Figure 8-6 The cut figure 8-5 Pythagorean triangle rearranged to demonstrate that it equals 6 squares

at either of your resulting triangles. Unlike many other objects and their areas, this calculation is visible: As if working a puzzle, can you see how each partial square matches with another partial square to make a whole, to equal six 1-inch squares? As shown in *Figure 8-6*, the fragments of squares 1 and 12 complete each other exactly, as do 2 and 11, and 6 and 7. Surprise numerical bonus: Each of these pairs adds up to 13. Shift the diagonal line to the other two corners, and the complimentary squares—4 and 9, 3 and 10, 6 and 7—will still add up to 13. Even if you number the squares vertically as columns, instead of as rows, this will still work, with the complimentary squares adding up to 13.

This triangle has another special trait: The sum of the squares of its two shorter sides (the 3 and the 4) is equal to the square of its long side (the 5). We can see this plain and clear in *Figure 8-7*. In the world of "real" math, this squaring trait is written $a^2 + b^2 = c^2$, or in this specific case $3^2 + 4^2 = 5^2$. To a math phobe like me, this looks less intimidating written as 3 x 3 plus 4 x 4 = 5 x 5. Surprise! In these numbers—9, 16, and 25-we find the dot-squares seen in *Figure 8-1* at the start of this chapter.

While the 3-by-4 rectangle we started with has none of the trick mathematical properties of magic squares, when its twelve numbers are added together, we see the total is 78, the number of cards in the Tarot deck: 1 + 2 + 3 + 4 + 5 + 6 + 7 + 8 + 9 + 10 + 11 + 12 = 78.

Remember this 3-by-4 rectangle and especially the Pythagorean triangle we get from it. We'll be seeing that triangle again.

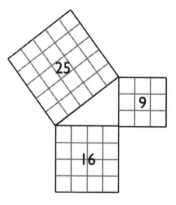

Figure 8-7 The dot patterns reappear in new form to define a Pythagorean triangle's edges

CHAPTER 9

Fibonacci, the Golden Ratio, and the Pentacle

The Fibonacci series isn't just some guy's arbitrary numbering scheme. It's the recognition that these numbers define spatial relationships occurring throughout nature, in what came to be called the Golden Ratio.

The numerical sequence's introduction to Europe is credited to Leonardo Fibonacci a.k.a. Leonardo of Pisa (circa 1170–circa 1240 CE). Raised in North Africa where his father ran a customs-house—counting was the family business—the young Fibonacci studied with Arabian mathematicians, then traveled extensively, always noticing how people made use of numbers. His book *Liber abaci (Book of the Abacus,* 1202 CE, in Latin) helped introduce many Arabic and Indian math concepts into European thought, including the decimal system and the Hindu-Arabic shapes we use to write the numbers.[1] Along with the Latin translation of al-Khwarizmi's *Arithmetic*, Fibonacci's work helped shape European thought.

In the Fibonacci series, each new number is the sum of the two previous numbers. So, start counting from 0. That's 0, 1. Add those together and you get 1 again, so the series becomes 0, 1, 1.

The new number—1—is added to the preceding number—1—so the series next reads 0, 1, 1, 2.

Add the newest final number—2—to its preceding 1 to get the next number: 3.

Whatever your final number is, add it to the number just ahead of it:

0, 1, 1, *2, 3* = 5
0, 1, 1, 2, *3, 5* = 8
0, 1, 1, 2, 3, *5, 8* = 13

Keep going, straight on 'til morning, and you've got the Fibonacci series: 0, 1, 1, 2, 3, 5, 8, 13, 21, 34, 55, 89, 144, 233, 377, 610, 987, 1597, 2584 and *onward ad infinitum.*

Any number in the Fibonacci series divided by the one right before it yields approximately 1.618 . . . (In a mathematical context, those final three dots mean these are "irrational" numbers that can't be resolved no matter how many digits follow the decimal point. *(Figure 9-1.)*

Likewise, any Fibonacci number divided by the one immediately *after* it yields approximately 0.618 . . . *(Figure 9-2.)*

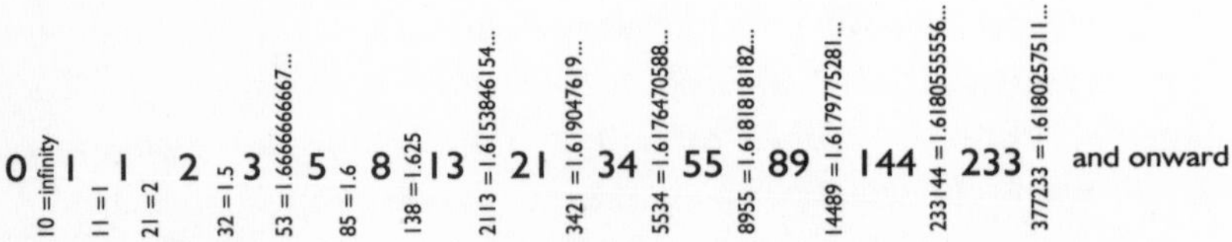

0 | 1 | 1 | 2 | 3 | 5 | 8 | 13 | 21 | 34 | 55 | 89 | 144 | 233 | and onward

1÷0 = infinity
1÷1 = 1
2÷1 = 2
3÷2 = 1.5
5÷3 = 1.6666666667...
8÷5 = 1.6
13÷8 = 1.625
21÷13 = 1.6153846154...
34÷21 = 1.61904761 9...
55÷34 = 1.6176470588...
89÷55 = 1.6181818182...
144÷89 = 1.617977528 1...
233÷144 = 1.6180555556...
377÷233 = 1.6180257511...

The magic number, 1.618 . . . Fibonacci sequence numbers, with each number divided by the adjacent smaller one to show how 1.618 . . . keeps appearing

Figure 9-1 Fibonacci graph 1.618

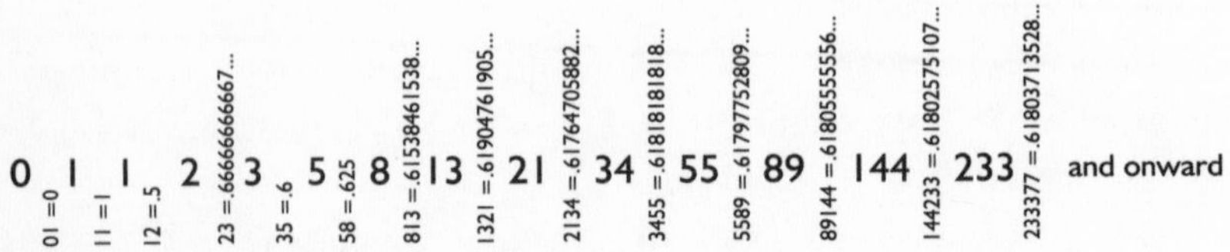

0 | 1 | 1 | 2 | 3 | 5 | 8 | 13 | 21 | 34 | 55 | 89 | 144 | 233 | and onward

0÷1 = 0
1÷1 = 1
1÷2 = .5
2÷3 = .6666666667...
3÷5 = .6
5÷8 = .625
8÷13 = .6153846 1538...
13÷21 = .6 190476 1905...
21÷34 = .6 1764705882...
34÷55 = .6 181818 18 18...
55÷89 = .6 179775 2809...
89÷144 = .6 1805555556...
144÷233 = .6 1802575 107...
233÷377 = .6 18037 13528...

The magic number, .618 . . . The sequence again, now with each number divided by the adjacent larger one to show how .618 . . . keeps appearing

Figure 9-2 Fibonacci graph 0.618

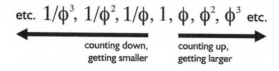

Figure 9-3 Counting Fibonacci

Your results will be least accurate with the smaller, single-digit Fibonacci numbers and increasingly precise as the numbers grow steadily larger. Those two key numbers—0.618 . . . and 1.618 . . .—are the proportional rates between parts of the Golden Ratio, going smaller to larger and vice versa. [2]

If you had plenty of math in school, you might want to skip ahead here. For those of us to whom this is indeed Greek, the *phi*-sign—Φ—is a means of expressing the Fibonacci/Golden Ratio relationships shown in the numbers. Above we divided, here we're multiplying. A series going from small-to-large might read like that in *Figure 9-3*. As written out—1, Φ, Φ^2, Φ^3—this secret code means that:

1 is the starting point in a Fibonacci series,

On the right, Φ is the first expression of the 1 x 1.618 . . . relationship,

Φ^2 is the second expression, Φ x 1.618 . . . and so on.

Each Φ symbol and accompanying number tells you how many steps into a Fibonacci series you've gone, expressing the relationship between sections rather than a specific inch or centimeter measurement. (When multiplying, don't include the . . . dots.) If your steps are getting smaller each time (as shown to the left of 1), the symbols will read like fractions—1/Φ means 1 x .618 . . .

Just decide what "1" is and then either count down in x .618 . . . increments, or count up in x 1.618 . . . increments.

The use of the Greek letter *phi* and the Φ are relatively new in this context, proposed early in the 20th century by American mathematician Michael Barr in honor of Phidias (c. 490-430 BCE), a Greek sculptor who reputedly based his work on the Golden Ratio. Prior to Barr's proposal, the Golden Ratio had been represented by the Greek letter T or *tau*, derived

Greek Tau sign

The Tau Cross

The Tau's short crossbar
matches the short "3" edge
of the Pythagorean triangle
and represents "1" in
the Golden Ratio

The Tau's long leg
matches the long "5" edge
of the Pythagorean triangle
and represents "φ" in
the Golden Ratio:
the crossbar's 1 x 1.618

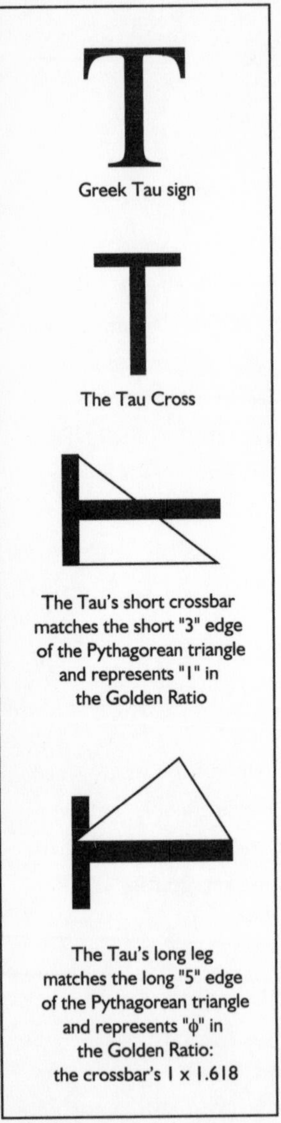

Figure 9-4 Tau and the triangle

from the Greek word *to-mi*, which actually means "the cut" or "the section." [3] As a pictorial representation of the Golden Ratio, τ makes better sense, and when written as a capital letter—T—closely expresses the actual measurements.

This is also the shape of the *tau* cross, which is something of a misnomer, since it's simply T-shaped and the two bars meet rather than cross each other. The *tau*-cross appears in some Tarot decks. Held by the *Emperor* on Major Arcana card #IV, it's capped with an orb for the effect of a scepter. Orb, sphere or simple circle, the combination of round shape with the *tau* T will reappear soon, with some surprises. *(Figure 9-4.)*

Use a sheet of graph paper to play further with Fibonacci relationships. One of the easiest graphics is simply to draw squares whose areas express the Fibonacci series, so that 1, 1, 2, 3, 5, etc. become a 1-by-1 square, another 1-by-1 square, a 2-by-2 square, a 3-by-3 square and so on. *(Figure 9-5.)* If you draw diagonal lines back through these squares, you'll find you've bisected your starting-point square, sometimes called the "eye," shown here in gray. *(Figure 9-6.)*

This all works with rectangular expressions of the Fibonacci-series numbers, too. Here your shapes are based on adjacent numbers in the Fibonacci series—1-by-1, 1-by-2, 2-by-3, 3-by-5, and so on. Again, each new rectangle fits neatly along the edges of those preceding it, and although your initial square is now in a different spot, your diagonal lines will again bisect it.

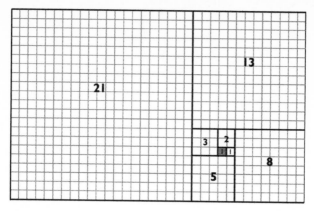

Figure 9-5 Building ever-larger squares with Fibonacci sequence numbers

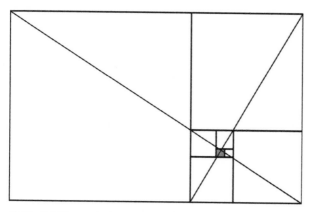

Figure 9-6 Diagonals drawn across the squares intersect in the first square, the "eye" in the arrangement

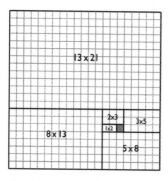

Figure 9-7 Here, adjacent Fibonacci numbers create rectangles that nest neatly against each other.

There's more. Next, still using the graph paper, draw a spiral, with each turn based on the Fibonacci numbers in sequence. *(Figure 9-9.)* This Fibonacci spiral springs rapidly out from its starting point, embodying Golden Ratio dimensions as it expands wildly, exuberantly, as if playing "crack the whip."

By way of contrast, draw another spiral, this time stepping out just one orderly row of squares at a time. This is the Archimedes spiral *(Figure 9-10.)*

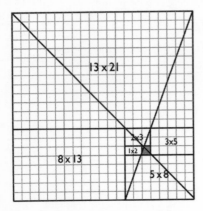

Figure 9-8 Diagonals drawn across the rectangles again intersect in the first square, the "eye" of this arrangement

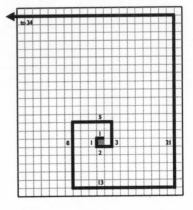

Figure 9-9 A spiral expanding in Fibonacci order

Figure 9-10 An Archimedes spiral expanding in orderly fashion

Figure 9-11 The dimensions of a clenched hand embody an expansive Fibonacci spiral

Things created by humans tend to follow the Archimedes spiral: Scrolls, the coil of clay or reed that begins a pot or basket, cinnamon rolls, paper towels, anything that gets rolled, coiled, or wound up. It's expanding, yes, but in the most orderly way possible, as the depth of each layer is based on the thickness of what's being rolled. Gravity and the materials are the determining factors for us. We're dealing with static materials and the layers need to rest against each other.

Mother Nature, however, creates with living material and has no such constraints. She works naturally and gracefully in the Fibonacci spiral, and She obligingly puts it everywhere. This spiral matches the curve of still-forming human and animal fetuses, and it matches the curl of the main muscle around the human heart.[4,5] It's found in seashells, like the one used as a trumpet by the dancing god Shiva to call forth creation. The petals on daisy-family flowers always equal a Fibonacci number, and the ratio of male to female bees in a hive is Fibonacci-based.[6] The pattern of seeds in a giant sunflower head follows two different Golden Ratio logarithmic spirals, as do the underlying designs in pinecones and pineapples. As plants grow and put out new leaves, the leaf placement will be Fibonacci based.[7] Golden Ratio measurements have been (and continue to be) intentionally incorporated into architecture, especially sacred architecture, inspiring everything from the size of the bricks to the overall proportions. When we curl our hands to grasp something, we form the Fibonacci spiral. *(Figure 9-11.)* These are just a few examples.

Figure 9-12 Fingertip-to-hand and onward, our bodies express Fibonacci proportions

Figure 9-13 The same Fibonacci proportions in a different gesture, expressed counting down from "1" instead of up

FIBONACCI'S HUMAN EMBODIMENT

You can use the Fibonacci numbers to create a pleasingly proportioned rectangle, a 5-by-8-foot area rug, for example. Of greater cosmic importance, the human figure echoes these Golden Ratio proportions.

This starts small, going from fingertip to knuckle, with each joint of the finger being proportionately about 1.618% larger. *(Figure 9-12.)* Measuring in the opposite direction, the numbering reverses. *(Figure 9-13.)*

To continue with the human form, the measurement from fingertip-to-wrist-bend times 1.618 will yield something like the distance from wrist-bend-to-elbow. And wrist-bend-to-elbow times 1.618 will give a measurement close to your individual elbow-to-fingertip cubit, which we met in Chapter 3.

Shifting around the body, measure from the ground between your feet (shoes off) up to your navel and multiply this number times 1.618. The total will be a close match for the distance across your body from fore-fingertip to fore-fingertip with arms outstretched, your personal fathom.

The proportional measurement underlying all of these things goes by many different names—Golden Ratio, Golden Mean, Golden Section, *aurea section* (Latin for golden section), the sacred cut, the golden cut, the Divine Proportion. The German term is *Goldene Schnitt*, which sounds like a cousin to Harry Potter's elusive Golden Snitch. [8]

Creating a Pentacle, Step-by-Step

The Fibonacci spiral can also spring from triangles nested within each other. *(Figure 9-14.)* By either name, *tau* or *phi*, the Golden Ratio is the foundation of the pentacle and is repeated throughout each pentacle, in shifting sizes, infusing the symbol at every step. *(Figure 9-15.)*

Figure 9-14 The Fibonacci spiral emerging from a Tau-based triangle

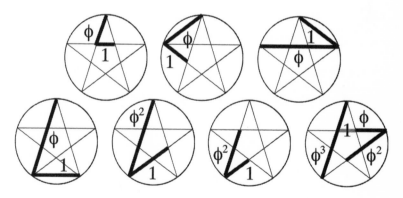

Figure 9-15 The Fibonacci-Golden Ratio proportions recurring—nonstop—throughout a pentacle

There's a way to create a pentacle with a simple building block we already met. Having played with the 3-4-5 triangle in Chapter 8's *Figure 8-4*, we'll now use ten of these shapes placed back to back to create a pentagon. *(Figure 9-16.)* This works because the short side of this triangle equals the short side of the *tau* (the "1" in the Golden Ratio) and the long side equals the long side of the *tau* (or *phi*, the "*Φ*" in the Golden Ratio), as shown in

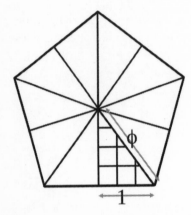

Figure 9-16 Building a pentagon from ten Pythagorean triangles

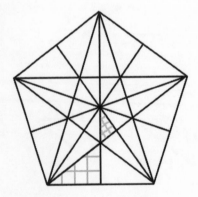

Figure 9-17 More lines are added to create other Pythagorean triangles throughout the pentagon

Figure 9-4. Remember, the triangle's edge measurements were 3 and 5, both Fibonacci numbers. Connect every other corner within this pentagon and you'll have a small pentacle. Add a few more lines and you'll see that you have new, smaller Pythagorean triangles throughout the pentagon. *(Figure 9-17.)*

But let's say we want a larger pentacle. Easily done, because a pentagon does something that a triangle or square—two-dimensional shapes with fewer sides—can only dream of.

If you extend lines outward along the edges of a square or triangle, you just get lines shooting out into space, since these lines never meet up with each other. But when you extend lines outward along the edges of a pentagon, the lines meet each other and create a new shape. Here's our pentacle. *(Figure 9-18.)* If you connect the new corner-points of this star with straight lines, you'll have a new pentagon. Encompass the star's points with a circle and you have a truly magical symbol embodying all these underlying harmonies of form and interconnection, the Emperor's circle-and-*tau*-sceptre united and transformed.

Back around 2400 BCE, the Babylonians defined the circle as 360°, based on their rough count of days in a year. Three-hundred-sixty is a wonderfully useful and versatile number, as the Babylonians—expert sky-watchers—knew. The math potential is vast, since 360 can be evenly divided by all twenty-two of the following numbers: 2, 3, 4, 5, 6, 8, 9, 10, 12, 15, 18, 20, 24, 30, 36, 40, 45, 60, 72, 90, 120 and 180.[9] (Hmm, twenty-two . . . that's the number of cards in the Tarot's Major Arcana.)

Dividing the circle into degrees allows us to mark longitude and latitude, and to delineate space astrologically. In combination with our pentacle, the circle also does its own set of curious math tricks. Divide a circle's 360 degrees by 5 (for the five points of the pentacle) and you'll get five sections of 72° each. *(Figure 9-19.)* Marked off around the circle's edge, these points are at 0°, 72°, 144°, 216°, 288° and back to 0°, also known as 360°. As we've done throughout the book, let's reduce these numbers. You'll see they all come out to 9.

If we rotate our star slightly, as if to make a ten-pointed star—simply done by straddling another 5-pointed star on top of our first one—the new

Figure 9-18 Extend the edge-lines of any simple pentagon and you'll create a pentacle

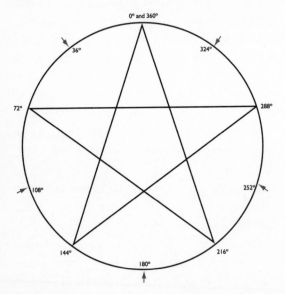

Figure 9-19 Within the 360° circle, the degrees on which this pentacle's points land all reduce to 9. Start at a different degree in the circle and you'll get a different result.

star's points will be at 36°, 108°, 180°, 252° and 324°. Again, each of these numbers reduces to 9.

Of course, you'd be correct in noting that these aren't the only numbers within 360° that will reduce to 9. Indeed, there are plenty of others. Pick any one of them—9 itself, for example. A star's points are 72° apart, so keep adding 72° to your starting point—9, 81, 153, 225 and 275—and you'll have another pentacle or pentagon with its corner-numbers reducing to 9.

But *any* five points separated around a circle by 72° will always yield a pentacle, so what of it? Aha! Whatever degree you start at, every angle in *that* pentacle will reduce to the same number:

1°, 73°, 145°, 217° and 289° all reduce to 1 (often via 10 or 19)

13°, 85°, 157°, 229° and 301° (all reduce to 4 (via 13)

This is true even when fractions are involved: Just treat them as individual digits when reducing them, ignoring the decimal point:

7.143°, 79.143°, 151.143°, 223.143° and 295.143° all reduce to 6 (via 15 or 24). Curious, eh? You can use this to personalize a pentacle, embedding a number significant to you—perhaps your birthday expressed as degrees and a fraction—and then moving forward in step of 72°. Circles and pentacles in combination are magical.

From Plants to Planets

In 1620, an elderly German woman named Katharina was charged with witchcraft. Like others arrested, she was an herbalist who knew the healing and magical properties of plants. And, also like others, gossip and personal grudges apparently helped provoke her arrest.

But unlike many others who were arrested and tortured, charges against Katharina were eventually dropped. Katharina's influential son helped win her freedom.

That son was Johannes Kepler (1571–1630), a German astronomer, math professor, and imperial mathematician to Rudolf II. Kepler's enduring fame rests on his three groundbreaking calculations of planetary motion, now known as "Kepler's laws." These radically innovative "laws" altered our understanding of the universe and are studied to this day.

Kepler himself was Christian, perhaps the only relatively safe route by which to study the stars. But the scientist was also a metaphysician. Kepler wrote eloquently about the number five, flowers, pentagons, and the Golden Ratio. He knew that the Divine Proportion—present in both fruit blossoms and pentagons—was a symbol of the divine creative spark wherever it appeared.[10]

As Kepler's mother certainly knew as an herbalist, many edible fruits do indeed begin as five-petalled blossoms. Some of Katharina's plant lore was also held by her mystic-mathematician son: It's mentioned in his writings. Did he learn of plants at his mother's knee, or independently? Did his plant awareness help fuel his scientific leaps of understanding? Crucially, it didn't prevent him from leaping. I choose to think it served as a springboard.

Like those two generations of Keplers, much of our own awareness straddles the smudged boundaries between ancient lore and modern science, the living pentacle we experience sensuously as an apple, alongside the pentacle we construct mathematically. Contradictory? Says who? We're simultaneously capable of vastly diverse modes of comprehension, multiple ways of knowing.

Let's move on to look at the celestial version of the magical pentacle shape.

CHAPTER 10

Venus' Pentacle

The planet Venus traces a pentacle in the sky, repeatedly, precisely and on a near-perfect schedule. Many early civilizations knew this—the Mayans and pre-Aztec Totonacs, the Egyptians, Sumerians, and Greeks.[1,2] The Knights Templar knew, too.[2,3]

Because they're both closer to the Sun than Earth is, Mercury and Venus never wander far from Sol. Astrologically, that means they never form wide aspects to the Sun: No oppositions (180° separation), trines (120°), or squares (90°) on any astrological charts. Mercury and Venus *never* oppose Sol. They're always near the Sun, "inner planets," inside our own orbit.

Small Mercury is often so near the Sun that our view of it is limited. Venus, by contrast, is beautiful, easily seen, and very obvious in its orbit. This is how that works.

Facing East: After disappearing from view for up to 14 days in her brief inferior conjunction, or "short encounter" *(*Number 1 in *Figure 10-1)*, Venus reappears as a brilliant predawn Morning Star (Number 2). Her first post-conjunction morning appearance is called the heliacal rising (from *helios*, Greek for "Sun"). Each day Venus separates farther, speeding out ahead of the dawn and moving far ahead of the Sun, 47° at most (Number 3). Then, after about eight months as a Morning Star, Venus gradually comes back close in line to the rising Sun (Number 4), and finally vanishes again, as her orbit takes her *behind* the Sun (Number 5).

Facing West: Venus remains out of sight for up to three months in her superior conjunction, or "long encounter" *(*Number 5 in *Figure 10-2)*, and then appears in the West as a bright Evening Star, first visible just after sunset. At first, she's low in the sky and sets soon after the Sun does (Number 6), but gradually she extends her sky-time. Again Venus widens her distance from Sol, up to 47° degrees of elongation (Number 7), lingering in view up to about 3 hours after the Sun has gone down. As Evening Star, she graces the night sky for roughly eight months, then eventually closes her gap with the Sun again. Moving *between* Earth and the Sun this time, she finally vanishes back into an inferior conjunction (Number 8), only to reappear shortly in the eastern predawn sky, a Morning Star again. *(*Number 1 in *Figure 10-1.)*

We don't see Venus at all during her conjunctions with the Sun. She's either conjunct the Sun and *behind* it—"superior conjunction" with the larger object in front—or conjunct the Sun and in *front* of it—"inferior conjunction" with the smaller planet in front. Our distant ancestors observed these matters carefully and found them absolutely fascinating.

We find Venus' star pattern the same way our distant ancestors did, by tracking her relation to the Sun with her rhythmic appearances and disappearances while simultaneously noting her position against the constellations of the zodiac.

Start to finish, the Venus-pentacle cycle takes 8 years, and she then returns to within 2°–3° of her starting point. (This equals 99 lunar cycles: see Number 8 in Chapter 11 on "Individual Numbers.") Visually, this can be tracked from just after the Sun-Venus inferior conjunction, when Venus first reappears in her heliacal rising as Morning Star. *(Figure 10-3.)* You can find the conjunction dates in an ephemeris—the average recurrence is every 584 days, which is Venus' synodic period, the time a planet takes to return to a specific place in relation to the Sun. On an astrological chart, mark out the locations of the inferior conjunctions (or superior—don't mix them!) in their chronological order and you'll see the pentagram. It appears the same way we naturally draw stars ourselves, with one continuous line, going crisscross, from point to every other point.

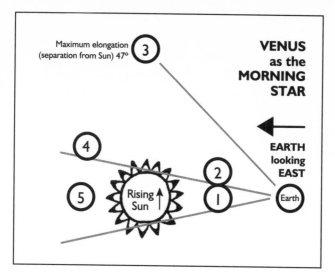

Figure 10-1 Venus as Morning Star

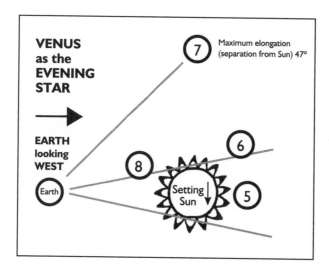

Figure 10-2 Venus as Evening Star

Did ancient people have the sky-knowledge necessary to track this? Absolutely. The Sumerians were the first people to identify the zodiacal constellations, as early as 2300 BCE.[4] From them the knowledge spread within their own Tigris-Euphrates region, then on to the Greeks, Egyptians, and others. Independently, the Maya arrived at vast knowledge of Venus and used it throughout their calendar system.

As we view all this from our own super-precise era, remember that the 584 days in this cycle is an average, not a guarantee. Dates and times in an ephemeris note the exact conjunctions, when Venus is most directly in line with the Sun. As with New Moons, that doesn't mean that Venus reappears immediately. If this is an inferior conjunction, she'll show up in the pre-dawn East a few days or a week later; if it's a superior conjunction, we may wait a month or more for her reappearance as Evening Star. The length of the wait is determined by where Earth and Venus each are in their own orbits and in relation to each other.

The dates given in the *Figure 10-3* are for exact inferior conjunctions, with Venus between Earth and the Sun. Venus also draws her star when making superior conjunctions *(Figure 10-4)*, but to track the pentacle cycle, pick either the inferior or superior conjunctions to track, or you'll get a pentagon instead of a pentacle.

A couple of final, factual points about Venus:

Daytime Venus: Venus is visible during the day. At the time of greatest elongation (so you needn't look too near the Sun), find her in the predawn sky against the dark backdrop of the night sky. Then you can continue to follow her course into the daylight hours, although she's much less visible then, since her brightness provides little contrast against pale daytime skies.

June 2012: During her inferior conjunction, Venus very occasionally lines up so precisely with the Sun that she actually crosses Sol's face. If this were our Moon instead of Venus, we'd have a solar eclipse. Venus makes this very precise alignment far less often than the Moon does, and what we see instead of an eclipse is a flurry of science articles in the newspapers. Lucky us, to live in interesting times: This very rare event occurred on June 8, 2004, and will happen again in June 2012, but then won't repeat again until December 2117, so see it in 2012 if you can.[5] Just as with solar eclipses, don't look directly at the Sun!

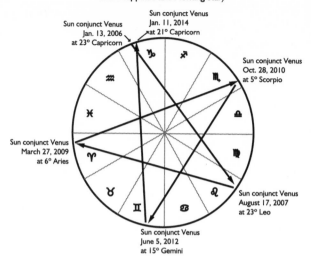

Inferior Conjunctions
(Venus moves in front of the Sun,
then reappears as a Morning Star)

Sun conjunct Venus
Jan. 13, 2006
at 23° Capricorn

Sun conjunct Venus
Jan. 11, 2014
at 21° Capricorn

Sun conjunct Venus
Oct. 28, 2010
at 5° Scorpio

Sun conjunct Venus
March 27, 2009
at 6° Aries

Sun conjunct Venus
August 17, 2007
at 23° Leo

Sun conjunct Venus
June 5, 2012
at 15° Gemini

Figure 10-3 Venus-Sun inferior conjunction

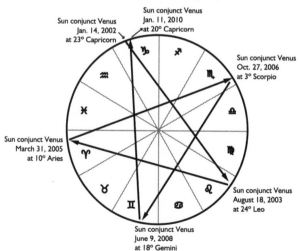

Superior Conjunctions
(Venus moves behind the Sun,
then reappears as an Evening Star)

Sun conjunct Venus
Jan. 14, 2002
at 23° Capricorn

Sun conjunct Venus
Jan. 11, 2010
at 20° Capricorn

Sun conjunct Venus
Oct. 27, 2006
at 3° Scorpio

Sun conjunct Venus
March 31, 2005
at 10° Aries

Sun conjunct Venus
August 18, 2003
at 24° Leo

Sun conjunct Venus
June 9, 2008
at 18° Gemini

Figure 10-4 Venus-Sun superior conjunction

CHAPTER 11

The Geometric Solids

The geometric "Platonic solids" are simple but significant shapes, three-dimensional, mathematically basic, beautiful, and profoundly symbolic. Greek philosopher Plato referred to geometric shapes in his *Timaeus*, equating them to the five elements—Earth, Air, Fire, Water, and Æther. Speaking metaphorically, Plato called these geometric shapes "the building blocks of creation," crediting their structural harmony with bringing order out of chaos. Because of their mention in *Timaeus*, these five forms are sometimes called the "Platonic solids," but that's misleading. Plato certainly didn't invent the shapes: Neolithic variations have been found in Britain, carved from rock and predating Plato by at least 1,000 years.[1,2]

The five polyhedrons (Greek *polus*, "many" + *hedra*, "face") that make up the group—tetrahedron, cube, octahedron, icosahedron, and dodecahedron—are unique for several reasons. Each is created by combining multiples of a single two-dimensional shape (triangle, square, or pentagon) of exactly the same size, so that each flat side—each face—is identical. It's as if each shape is a 3-D puzzle built from exactly identical pieces. The tetrahedron is the simplest of the shapes. Its four faces are the minimum among geometric solids: With fewer than four faces, a shape would either be two-dimensional—flat—rather than three-dimensional, or be open on one side and hence not "solid." Belief held that "open" forms let malevolent influences enter—like leaving your door unlocked, or in metaphysical terms, failing to cast a complete circle—hence the preference for nonporous, "solid" forms, closed along all the edges and sides.

Artists have played extensively with the geometric solids and other polyhedron forms. Albrecht Dürer included a complex geometric solid in his etching *Melencolia (Figure 5-9)*, with at least two different 2-D shapes used as faces. Dutch artist M. C. Escher (1898–1972) used the Platonic solids repeatedly. Among those that appear in his prints are a dodecahedron (twelve-sides), interlaced tetrahedrons and cubes, stellar dodecahedrons and more, all presented in the most eye-boggling manner. An ocean-themed icosahedron (twenty-sided) candy box that Escher designed for a *chocolaterie* featured a five-legged starfish curving around each five-edged vertex (meaning corner). Like Dürer, Escher was a printmaker and originally created each image in reverse, a perspective shift that sparks corresponding shifts in perception.

In 2003, a team of French and U.S. scientists studying signals from a microwave satellite came to the theory (promptly challenged by other scientists) that the universe was not only finite, but—far stranger—shaped like a dodecahedron.[3] When you look at this shape, try imagining the entire universe on the inside of the dodecahedron shape. Now try to picture the next part of their theory: Faces of the dodecahedron that are opposite each other are related in such a way that a spaceship flying "out" through a face on one side would simultaneously reenter through the corresponding face on the other side. Besides what this could do for travel, the science fiction possibilities are magnificent!

The solids are represented in *Figures 11-1* through *11-5*.

Tetrahedron

Greek *tetra*, "four" + *hedra*, "face"

Created from 4 equilateral triangles = 4 faces

Total edges = 6

Length of edges = $\sqrt{2}$

Vertices = 3 edges meet at each vertex

Total number of vertices = 4

Symbolism

Element: Fire
Season: Summer
Symbolic attributes: Willpower, courage and passion, self-definition
In human physiology: Electric impulses in the brain and heart
Sense: Sight
In Nature: Lightning, stars, volcanoes, high noon
Astrologically: Aries, Leo, and Sagittarius, the Fire Signs

Figure 11-1a Tetrahedron from the top

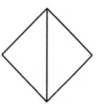

Figure 11-1b Tetrahedron turned to a ¾ angle

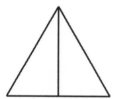

Figure 11-1c Tetrahedron from the side

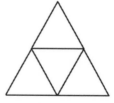

Figure 11-1d Tetrahedron opened out flat

Cube

Greek *kubos*, "six-sided cube"
Created from 6 equal squares = 6 faces
Total edges = 12
Length of edges = 1
Vertices = 3 edges meet at each vertex
Total number of vertices = 8

Symbolism

Element: Earth

Season: Winter

Symbolic attributes: Stability, power, manifestation, physical actions

In human physiology: Body, flesh and bones

Sense: Touch

In Nature: Earth herself; soil, rocks and plants, deepest night

Astrologically: Capricorn, Taurus, and Virgo, the Earth Signs

Figure 11-2a Cube from the top

Figure 11-2b Cube turned to a ¾ angle

Figure 11-2c Cube from the side

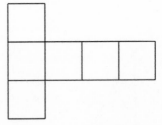

Figure 11-2d Cube opened out flat

Octahedron

Greek *okta*, "eight" + *hedra*, "face"

Created from 8 equilateral triangles = 8 faces

Total edges = 12

Length of edges = $\sqrt{\frac{1}{2}}$

Vertices = 4 edges meet at each vertex

Total number of vertices = 6

Symbolism

Element: Air
Season: Spring
Symbolic attributes: Intellect, inspiration, new beginnings, mental activities
In human physiology: Breath
Sense: Smell
In Nature: Wind, clouds, high peaks and windy plains, dawn
Astrologically: Libra, Aquarius, and Gemini, the Air Signs

Figure 11-3a Octahedron from the top

Figure 11-3b Octahedron turned to a ¾ angle

Figure 11-3c Octahedron from the side

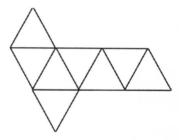

Figure 11-3d Octahedron opened out flat

Icosahedron

Greek *eikosi,* "twenty" + *hedra,* "face"
Created from 20 equilateral triangles = 20 faces
Total edges = 30
Length of edges = Φ
Vertices = 5 edges meet at each vertex
Total number of vertices = 12

Symbolism

Element: Water
Season: Autumn
Symbolic attributes: Emotion, dreams, intuitions
In human physiology: Blood, tears, all body fluids
Sense: Taste
In Nature: Oceans, streams, rain, all waters, evening
Astrologically: Cancer, Scorpio, and Pisces, the Water Signs

Figure 11-4a Icosahedron from the top

Figure 11-4b Icosahedron turned to a ¾ angle

Figure 11-4c Icosahedron from the side

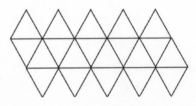

Figure 11-4d Icosahedron opened out flat

Dodecahedron

Greek *dodeka*, "twelve" + *hedra*, "face"
Created from 12 pentagons = 12 faces
Total edges = 30
Length of edges = 1/Φ
Vertices = 3 edges meet at each vertex
Total number of vertices = 20

Symbolism

Element: Spirit/Ether
Symbolic attributes: Divine connection, immanence
In human physiology: Spirit, soul
Sense: Hearing
In Nature: Space, the heavens
Astrological symbolism: The full zodiac

Figure 11-5a Dodecahedron from the top

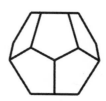

Figure 11-5b Dodecahedron turned to a ¾ angle

Figure 11-5c Dodecahedron from the side

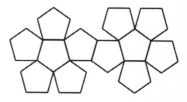

Figure 11-5d Dodecahedron opened out flat

Things to Do with the Geometric Solids

Drawing geometric solids on paper is interesting, but seeing them three-dimensionally is what really brings them to life and shows their clear, clean beauty to best advantage. Here are a few suggestions for doing this:

1. Make some. Drinking straws and string (plus patience) can do the trick for some of the solids. Whichever shape you intend to make, all the straws must be the same length. A piece of craft wire to act as either needle or hook will make threading your string much easier. The advantage here is that you can see all the lines of each hollow form. They're lightweight, too. Hang some from the ceiling for your contemplative pleasure. The trick is that some—like the tetrahedron—are "rigid," meaning they'll hold their shape, while others—like the cube—will collapse like wobbled-leg card tables. Yikes! Have fun! Need more of a challenge? Try this in miniature using bugle beads.

2. Find a set. A few years ago, I was gifted with a set of solids carved in quartz crystal, each is a little over one-inch high. They're very elegant and their transparency allows for viewing from a variety of angles to really examine their forms. And they can't collapse. If these sound intriguing, look for them at metaphysical stores, rock shops, or gem-and-mineral shows.

3. Find a kit. Museum gift shops, nature stores, and any place that sells the more exploratory types of toys may stock kits for assembling the geometric solids. You can also find some online at *www.polygon.com*.

CHAPTER 12

Individual Numbers

We find three Norns mentioned in one book, thirteen treasures of Britain in another.

Over the years, I've found tiny references to numbers and their assorted spiritual associations throughout countless books, like numerical needles in library-sized haystacks. What if there could be lots of information about lots of numbers all in one place? It wouldn't have to be the ultimate, all-inclusive compilation of metaphysical number lore, but it could be a starting point. Something like this . . .

Some Things about 0

- A Fibonacci series number (see Chapter 9)
- *Tarot:* Card 0, the Fool—One theory of the Tarot's origins is that all the vital knowledge of the ancient world was codified into the cards so it wouldn't be lost. This may never be proven true or false, but a number of possible "coincidences" are contained in the cards, and there are probably many others waiting to be discovered.
- A dot or point is zero-dimensional
- *Word origin*: Our word *zero* comes from the Arabic *sifr*, also the root of our word *cipher*.[1] Other sources identify the Arabic word for the zero as *tziphra* or *zephirum*, while the Hebrew word for zero is *sifra*, meaning "void."[2]

- Along with 1, 0 is the basis of all binary-based computer communications.
- We shape a zero with thumb and index finger, leaving three fingers free, as in *Figure 12-1*. *Kaph*, the Hebrew letter for the *K* sound, also means "the hollow of the hand" and the early symbol for the letter *K* looks like those three spare fingers. Was this zero-and-empty-hand gesture the origin of "OK" to signal "I'm holding nothing—I'm not a threat—My hand is open and I'm ready to receive new experiences!"?
- *Synonyms:* Mathematically, zero doesn't mean "nothing," but that's often what we mean by "zero" when we're speaking. Other synonyms for that usage: nil, nada, zip, zilch, naught, nix, cipher, blank, scratch, void, "goose egg" (shaped like 0), nothingness, nullity, vacuity, "plenty o' nuttin" (Gershwin), blank slate, *tabula rasa* (meaning "erased tablet").

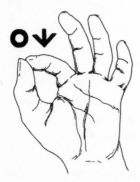

Figure 12-1 Hand making "Okay" sign

Some Things about 1

- A Fibonacci series number
- First of the prime numbers, which through multiplication can only be reached by 1 (1 x themselves), and which are divisible only by 1 or by themselves.
- *Tarot:* Card I, the Magician and also, by reduction, Card X, the Wheel of Fortune and Card XIX, the Sun. In Tarot it's often useful to reduce the Major Arcana cards to single digit numbers to explore unifying themes.
- One-line shapes are circles and ovals and the lemniscate (sideways-8), shown in *Figure 12-2*. In the Indian Tattva symbols, a blue circle means

Air, and a violet oval means Æther or Spirit. Representative sounds for Air are the whispery sound made by brushing the fingers across a drumhead (which can be written as *cha*) and the metallic ring of a tambourine's jingles.[3]

Figure 12-2 Lemniscate

- *Word origin:* Middle English on from Old English *an*; akin to German *ein*, Latin *unus*, Greek oine, and Sanskrit *eka*
- A line or curve is one-dimensional. Spirals are single-line open forms.
- As mentioned in "Some Things about 0," 0 and 1 are the basis of all binary-digit-based computer communications. My personal binary symbols: a frame drum (0) and a beater-stick (1).
- Create a Mobius strip. *(Figure 12-3.)* Cut one strip of paper about 1 inch wide and 12-14 inches long. Bring the narrow ends together to form a circle, but before joining them with tape or staple, flip one end over, so the narrow "front" of one end meets the narrow "back" of the other. You'll end up with a paper loop with a twist in it. When you lay it down on the table, it will naturally try to take a figure-8 shape. Now the cool part: Draw one line down the long middle of the strip, without lifting the pencil from the paper. You'll eventually return to your starting point, but your pencil line will be on both sides of the paper. As you see, the Mobius strip acts as if it has only one side. Flatten it out *(Figure 12-4)* and you'll see the origin of the recycle symbol. *(Figure 12-5.)*
- The first chakra is the root, at the spine's base. Its symbolic color is red, and it fuels our consciousness of basic survival issues—food, shelter, safety. A more comprehensive symbol is a yellow square (representing the Earth element) within a four-petalled lotus.

Figure 12-3 Mobius strip

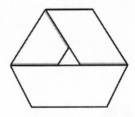

Figure 12-4 Mobius strip flattened

Figure 12-5 Recycle symbol

- *Synonyms and related words:* Uno, lone, only, solo, singular, ace, unit, monad, sole, solitary, individual, odd, onliest, uni-
- Can symbolize beginnings, self, ideas, unity, gifts, seeds, potential, initiation, isolation

Some Things about 2

- A Fibonacci-series number
- A prime number (in fact, the *only* prime number that's also an even number). Remember, prime numbers are those that through multiplication can only be reached by 1 (1 x themselves), and which are divisible only by 1 or by themselves. Since all higher even numbers can be multiplied and divided by 2, none of them beyond 2 are prime numbers. The "Sieve of Eratosthenes" technique eliminates non-prime numbers: Count forward from prime-2, crossing out each second number (4, 6, 8, and so on) because these would be divisible by 2. Repeat this elimination from 3,

crossing out every third number (that is, 6, 9, 12, 15, and so on) and onward through the numbers. Those remaining are primes.[4] Add together the primes that appear in the Tarot's Major Arcana—1, 2, 3, 5, 7, 11, 13, 17, and 19—and the total is 78, the number of cards in the full Tarot deck.

- *Tarot:* Card II, the High Priestess (also, when reduced, Card XI, Justice and Card XX, Judgment)

- Closed shapes drawn with two lines are the heart, the *vesica piscis* (the shape between two half-overlapped circles, shown in *Figure 12-6),* the crescent, and the *mandorla* (Italian, "almond"). In the Tattva system, a silver crescent stands for Water. A representative sound for Water is a deep and vibrating drumbeat, written as *dum.*

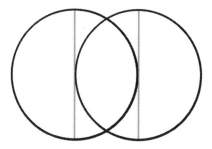

Figure 12-6 *Vesica piscis*

- A plane or surface is two-dimensional. A painting is two-dimensional (or 2-D) art since it can be measured only two ways, by height and by width. (An artwork's meaning, one sincerely hopes, is beyond measure.)

- *Word origin:* Middle English from Old English *twa,* akin to German *zwei,* Latin *duo,* Greek *duo,* and Sanskrit *dva*

- When elongated, the *vesica piscis* becomes the shape of a weaver's shuttle, the tool that carries the weft yarn back and forth between the warp threads. The French word for shuttle, *navette,* is also the name for a bread roll in this shape eaten at Candlemas in honor of the Black Madonna.[5] Many goddesses are credited with "weaving" fate. The *vesica piscis* also represents the shape of the vulva or *yoni,* our doorway into life.

- Birds are born twice—first as an egg, then as the hatchling that emerges. This makes the egg an excellent symbol for rebirth.
- A horizontal *vesica piscis* is the Egyptian hieroglyph symbolizing "mouth," or more specifically, the mouth of Ra. This is also the curved shape of a vibrating string.[6] The cosmic energy of life is often described as a vibration, a nonverbal sound, so there's the implicit idea here that Ra called life into being.
- The number 2 represents duality, which we experience when we see ourselves reflected in a mirror or water. Some Moon-related deities are depicted holding mirrors. Does this express an early understanding that the Moon simply reflects the light of the Sun?
- The second chakra is in the navel area. Its symbolic color is orange, and it governs our vitality. Its more comprehensive symbol is a white Crescent Moon (representing water) within a six-petalled lotus.
- *Synonyms and related words:* Dual, twain, twine (two strands of cord twisted together), entwine, twice, couple, doublet, dyad, deuce, pair, twins, match, both, dual, duplicity, duo-, bi-, bicycle. *Biscotti* (Italian) and *zweiback* (German) both refer to crisp twice-baked breads.[7]
- Can symbolize balance, duality, "other," opposites, choice, reflection, subconscious, nurturing

Some Things about 3

- Both a Fibonacci series number and a prime number
- *Tarot:* Card III, the Empress (also, when reduced, Card XII, the Hanged Man and Card XXI, the World)
- A closed shape you can draw with three lines is any triangle. In the Tattva, an even-sided, upward-pointing red triangle signifies Fire. A representative sound for Fire is a sharp, ringing drumstroke, higher in pitch, played along the drum's rim and written as *tak*.
- The Square of Saturn is an order-3 square.
- *Word origin:* Middle English from Old English *ori*, akin to German *drei*, Latin *tres*, Greek *treis*, and Sanskrit *tri*
- Early on, "three" was a tricky concept. Some languages counted "1, 2, many," lacking specific number-words to refer to more than two. Two

embodies duality, while three embodies plurality, a significant shift of perception and possibility.[8]

- The Triple Goddess as Maiden, Mother, and Crone
- The Triple God as Youth, Hunter, and Sage
- Many religions perceive their divinities in trinities, for example, Isis, Osiris, and Horus (Egyptian); Anu, Enlil, and Ea (Sumerian); Sin, Shamash, and Ishtar (Babylonian); Father, Son, and Holy Spirit Sophia (Christian); Creator Brahma, Preserver Vishnu, and Destroyer Shiva (Hindu); Banba, Futla, and Éire (Irish sovereignty); Selene (Moon), Diana (Earth), and Hecate (Underworld) (Greek); Zeus, Athena, and Apollo (Homeric Greek); Ptah, Sekhmet, and Nefetum (Egyptian); Thrice-born Dionysus.
- The "Three Maries of Provence" are celebrated in a huge Romany festival in Arles in the south of France from May 24 to May 28. The site is also called the "Les-Saintes-Maries-de-le-Mer," as this is the fabled spot where Mary Magdalene, two other Marys (mothers of disciples James the Greater and James the Less), and their traveling companions came to shore when they fled following Christ's crucifixion. The focus of the Romany festival is a black statue of Sara the Egyptian, or Sara-la-Kali, identified as either the servant or the daughter of Mary Magdalene. The figure is carried in procession from her church crypt down to the sea, immersed in the water, and then carried back.[9]
- At the solstices, the Sun "stands still" for 3 days before resuming its motion.
- Three Graces: Aglaia (Brilliant), Euphrosyne (Heart's Joy), and Thalia (Flower-Bringer)[10]
- Three Gorgons: Medusa, Euryale, and Sthenno
- Three pre-Islamic Arabian goddesses were Al-Lat (ruling fertility), Q're (the Virgin), and Al-Uzza ("Powerful One"), in a triad called *Manat*, for the Threefold Moon.[11]
- In the Babylonian version of the flood legend, the boatman Utnapishtim released three birds—a dove, a raven, and a swallow—to search for dry land.[12]
- Three Fates: Clotho spins life's thread, Lachesis measures it, and Atropos cuts it.

- Three Norns who, like the Fates, determine human destiny. The *Prose Edda* identified them as High-One, Just-As-High, and Third. Elsewhere, their names are given as Urth (Fate), Verthandi (Being), and Skuld (Necessity).[13]
- Three cheers, three bears, three little pigs, three wishes, "Good things come in threes," three blind mice, Three Wise Men, Three Stooges, Three Musketeers, "Easy as 1, 2, 3," three billy goats' gruff, three strikes, "Three's lucky"
- Three primary colors: In light, that means red, green, and blue-violet, while in pigment, it's red, blue, and yellow.
- Three encompasses all concepts of time—past, present, and future.
- The ancient Egyptians divided their year into three seasons: Inundation (time for sowing), Coming-Forth (growing), and Summer (the harvest time).
- Three-faced Hecate, goddess of crossroads, especially where three roads or pathways meet in a Y-shape called a *trivia*, meaning *tri* (three) and *via* (road).
- Three-headed Cerberus, the dog guarding the Underworld's gates
- A period of three days was considered the maximum length of a shamanic journey from which the practitioner could successfully return. Coincidentally, Jesus lay three days in the tomb and Jonah spent 3 days in the whale's belly—shamanic connotations? Also, there are three main realms in shamanic journeying: the Upper World, the Middle World, and the Lower World.
- *Triskelion:* A design with three spirals, or branches, or stylized legs or arms radiating from a common center point. *(Figure 12-7.)*
- The space we occupy—height, weight, and depth—is three-dimensional (3-D). In art, sculpture is three-dimensional.
- The classic 3-D glasses, with one red lens and one green lens, can give the illusion of depth to flat, 2-D surfaces.
- The tripod: Three is the right number of legs for an object to stand in a stable manner. A four-legged chair or table may be uneven and wobbly, but three-legged furniture will stand steady. Shakespeare's "three weird sisters," the three witches in *Macbeth*.
- The Moon looks full for three days and disappears as dark for three days.[14]

- Three modes in astrological signs: Cardinal (Aries, Cancer, Libra, and Capricorn); Fixed (Taurus, Leo, Scorpio, and Aquarius); and Mutable (Gemini, Virgo, Sagittarius, and Pisces)

Figure 12-7 Triskelion

- Three kinds of natural light: daylight, night (Moon, stars, or fully dark), and the transitional light of twilight
- Among some of North America's native people, corn, bean, and squash were referred to as the "three sisters." These food staples were often grouped together when planted.
- Three coins are used to read the *I Ching*.
- Three realms: Sky/Heaven/Realm of the Gods (rules over birth), Earth (rules over life) and the Underworld (rules over death)[15]
- As Jimi Hendrix eloquently pointed out, Earth is the "third stone from the sun.[16]
- The third chakra is that of the solar plexus. Its color is yellow and it affects our psychological being, our identity. Its more comprehensive symbol is a red triangle (representing fire) within a ten-petalled lotus.
- *Synonyms and related words:* Trio, triplet, threesome, triad, trinity, tri- (three or thirds), trey, thrice, triptych, tripartate, triskelion, triune, tricycle, trident, tripod, the "eternal triangle"
- Can symbolize synthesis, understanding, beauty, harmony, idealization, completion, growth

Some Things about 4

- *Tarot:* Card IV, the Emperor (also, when reduced, Card XIII, Death and the Fool, card 0 treated as number 22)
- Closed shapes you can draw with four lines are the square, and its stretched-out variations, the rectangle and the diamond. In the Tattva system, a yellow square stands for Earth. A representative sound for Earth is a drumstroke that strikes the drum's head and then rests there, stopping—"grounding"—the vibration. It's written as *kah*.
- The Square of Jupiter is an order-4 square.

- *Word origin:* Middle English from Old English *feower*, German *vier*, Latin *quattuor*, Greek *tettares*, and Sanskrit *catur*
- Four cardinal directions: east, south, west and north, the four corners of the Earth; and four other directions: above, below, around, and within
- Four is the smallest number you can use to create a "solid"object that is three-dimensional or free-standing.
- Four elements: Earth, Air, Fire, Water
- Four seasons: Spring, Summer, Autumn, and Winter
- Four "rounds" in a sweat lodge
- The human tongue can taste only four flavors: salt, sour, sweet, and bitter. The subtleties we perceive come from complex combinations of these four tastes.
- Tetramorphs are mythical beasts combining four creatures into one, often human, ram or bull, eagle, and lion, as implied on the Tarot's Wheel of Fortune and World cards.
- Freya traded four nights of lovemaking to four different dwarf craftsmen to acquire Brisingamen, her magical necklace.
- The fourth dimension: the 3-D group—height, weight, depth—plus time
- "One for the money, two for the show, three to get ready, and four to *go!*"
- Four ages of human life: infancy, childhood, adulthood, and elder years
- The fourth chakra is the heart chakra. Symbolically green in color, it works to harmonize the "higher" mind and emotions, that is, sympathy, kindness, empathy. Its more comprehensive symbol is a six-pointed star (two triangles overlapped) within a twelve-petalled lotus.
- *Synonyms and related words:* tetrad, quartet, quad-, tetra-, quart (4 cups), quadrant (for measuring the altitude of planets and stars, named because it divided the circle of space into fourths)
- Can symbolize stability, actualization, grounding, tradition, material world, reason, foundations

Some Things about 5

- Both a Fibonacci series number and a prime number
- *Tarot:* Card V, The Hierophant (also, when reduced, Card XIV, Temperance)

- Closed shapes you can draw with five lines are pentacles and pentagons.
- The Square of Mars is an order-5 square.
- *Word origin:* Middle English from Old English *fif*; akin to German *fünf*, Latin *quinque*, Greek *pente*, and Sanskrit *pañca*
- Five senses: Sight, smell, taste, touch, and hearing
- Five fingers, five toes
- Fifth dimension: Something beyond height, width, depth, and time/duration.
- Five elements in the classical Chinese system: Wood, Earth, Fire, Metal, and Water. These are depicted on some acupuncture charts as a pentacle.
- The rose portrayed in mystical tradition is the five-petalled *rosa canina*, or dog rose.[17] This is a basic rose, a wild rose, the shape of roses before they were extensively cultivated to have more petals and be flower-show huge. The five-petal shape, surrounding the sunlike yellow stamens in the center, is equated with the planet Venus' star-orbit. *(Figure 12-8.)* Additionally, each individual petal is roughly heart-shaped, appropriate to Venus' symbolism. Many other flowers associated with love also have five petals, and many plants and trees sacred to the goddess have five-lobed leaves: ivy, vine, cinquefoil, bramble (raspberry), fig, and plane tree (sycamore).[18]

Figure 12-8 Dog rose pentacle

- The *riq*, a Middle Eastern tambourine, has five groups of jingles (set as double pairs) spaced pentagonally around its rim. An instrument with deep ceremonial roots, the tambourine combines two important ancient instruments, the sistrum and the drum.[19]

- The number 5 symbolizes Mayan deity Quetzalcoatl, who in myth returned from the Underworld on the fifth day, a possible metaphor for the time planted corn takes to sprout shoots.[20]
- The quintessential or quintessence, now used to mean "the ultimate," literally means the fifth essence, or fifth element, referring to the complete sacred combination of Earth, Air, Fire, Water, and Spirit.
- The fifth chakra is in the throat. Its symbolic color is blue and it is the center of spiritual/religious instinct and healing that draws on these. Its more comprehensive symbol is a white circle within a sixteen-petalled lotus. A representative sound for Ether is the ringing tone of a high-pitched bell.
- *Synonyms and related words:* Quintet, quintuplet, cinque, pentagram, "fin" (slang: a human "fin" has five fingers), pentad, quin-, quint-, pent-, vee (slang from the Roman numeral V for 5)
- Can symbolize creativity, conflict, challenge, stagnation, desire, adaptation, obstacles, bridges, midpoints

Some Things about 6

- *Tarot:* Card VI, the Lovers (also, when reduced, Card XV, the Devil)
- Closed shapes drawn with six lines are the hexagon and the Star of David or Seal of Solomon (two overlapped triangles, upward-pointing for male, downward-pointing for female, a mystical symbol of divine balance)
- The Square of the Sun is an order-6 square.
- *Word origin:* Middle English from Old English *siex;* akin to German *sechs,* Latin *sex,* Greek *hex,* and Sanskrit *sas.*
- The Square of the Sun's total number is 666, said to be the measurement in feet of the labyrinth's walkway at Chartres Cathedral and a number sacred to Aphrodite.[21]
- Each cell of a honeycomb has six sides, a wonderfully compact and efficient use of space. Draw a hexagon by extending the *vesica piscis (Figure 12-6)* with another circle, then connecting the angles. *(Figure 12-9.)*
- The sixth sense: Perception beyond and independent of the other five senses

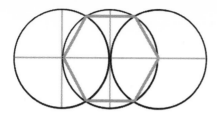

Figure 12-9 Drawing a hexagon

- The Latin word for "six" was *sex*—does our own English word *sex* relate back to the number 6? Remember, in the Tarot's Major Arcana, the Lovers card is Number VI. (See "Some Things about 13.")
- Six lines to each hexagram in the *I Ching*.
- Six is a pervasive number in the substructure of minerals.[22]
- The sixth chakra is in the brow, in the area of the pineal gland. This area is also called "the third eye." Its color is indigo and it is transcendental, ruling the higher aspirations of the soul, as does the crown chakra. (See "Some Things about 7.") Its more comprehensive symbol is the Sanskrit symbol for *Aum* (representing light) within a two-petalled lotus.
- *Synonyms and related words:* Hexad, sextet, sextuplet, hexagon, hex-, sext-, sextant (for measuring the altitude of planets and stars, named because it divided the circle of space into sixths)
- Can symbolize exuberance, mercy, justice, love, divine power, wisdom, perfection, majesty

Some Things about 7

- A prime number
- *Tarot:* Card VII, the Chariot (also, when reduced, Card XVI, the Tower)
- The Square of Venus is an order-7 square.
- *Word origin:* Middle English from Old English *seofon*, German *sieben*, Latin *septem*, Greek *hepta*, and Sanskrit *sapta*
- Seven lines can create a seven-rayed star. Also, a triangle (3 = synthesis) above a square (4 = stability) forms the simplest visual and metaphorical representation of a home, the same way that little kids often draw houses.

- The Pythagoreans are said to have paid special attention to 7, believing that dates that were divisible by 7—7, 14, 21, 28—were likely to be important.[23]
- Seven colors in the spectrum: Red, orange, yellow, green, blue, indigo, violet
- Seventh heaven, seven years of bad luck, seventh son of a seventh son
- Seven Pleiadian stars: Alcyone, Calaeno, Electra, Maia, Merope, Asterope, Taygete
- Seven stars each in the Big and Little Dippers
- Woden killed the giant Ymir and cut him into seven pieces to create Earth and Sky.[24]
- Seven chakras, focal points of specific energy in the human body
- Seven golden braids on Celtic fairy-seer Feithline, who foretold Queen Maeve's approaching death[25]
- Seven rungs on the ladder to enlightenment. In ascending order, the rungs are made from lead, tin, iron, copper, gold, mercury, and silver.[26] (Unless they're in a different order: No two sources seem to agree on the metals or their arrangement, but there are consistently seven rungs.)
- Plutarch wrote of an Egyptian Winter Solstice ritual called "Seeking for Osiris": A golden cow statue, symbolizing Isis and draped with black cloth, was carried seven times around a statue of Osiris.[27]
- Seven "deadly sins, seven virtues, seven liberal arts, Snow White and the Seven Dwarves
- The seven gates Inanna passed on her Underworld journey. The "dance of the seven veils" may have been a metaphoric retelling of her epic descent, in some versions of which she bartered away seven articles of dress to seven gatekeepers for safe passage.[28,29]
- "In our every deliberation, we must consider the impact of our decisions on the next seven generations" (from the Great Law of the Iroquois Confederacy)
- Of the astrological aspects, only the Septile—one-seventh of 360°—is calculated using a fraction: $360 \div 7 = 51.42857\ldots$ Astrologically, it's written as $51°25'$
- Seven orifices in the human head: two nostrils, two eyes, two ears, and one mouth

- "A lie has seven endings"—a Swahili proverb[20]
- The seven notes of the diatonic scale: C D E F G A B
  (Maybe this scale was used by ancient Sumerians, maybe it was invented by Pythagoras. However it evolved, the diatonic scale has five whole tones [W] and two half-tones [H] arranged as WWHWWWH, or what we now warble as Do-Re-Mi-Fa-So-La-Ti. Stop there! The final Do we're accustomed to hearing comes a bit later in this chapter.)
- The Aztec goddess of corn and other grains was named Chicomecoatl, which means "Seven Snakes."[31]
- The Babylonian creation myth *Enuma Elish* speaks of seven winds, seven spirits of the storm, seven evil diseases, and seven divisions of the Underworld behind seven doors closed by seven seals.[32]
- Seshet, the Egyptian goddess of writing, mathematics, and architecture. Alternative spellings of her name included *Sefhet*, meaning seven. In some representations, the star or flower over her head looks eight-pointed, but in better-preserved carvings, we see that only seven are petals. *(Figure 12-10.)* The lowest "south-pointing" ray is clearly shaped like a reed pen, its point resting just over Seshet's head. Are those really inverted cow horns over her head, or is that a primitive caliper for measuring? Her tiger-skin garment symbolizes the starry sky, since Egyptian ceremonial buildings were aligned to the stars with Seshet's help.[33]

- The crown chakra, in the dome of the head, includes the pituitary gland. Its color is violet and it is transcendental, ruling the higher aspirations of the soul, as does the brow chakra. (See "Some Things about 6.") This affects abilities such as clairvoyance, spiritual intuition, and healing. The crown chakra's more comprehensive symbol is a lotus with 1,000 (or innumerable) petals.

Figure 12-10 Seshet

- *Synonyms and related words:* Heptad, heptagon, septet, September (dating from the time when March was considered the first month), heptahedron (a seven-faced shape), hep-, hepta, sept-
- Can symbolize reflection, preparation, independence, discipline, inner work

Some Things about 8

- A Fibonacci-series number
- *Tarot:* Card VIII, Strength or Justice (also, when reduced, Card XVII, the Star)
- A closed shape you can draw with eight lines in an octagon
- The Square of Mercury is an order-8 square (like the 64-cell chess- or checkerboard)
- *Word origin:* Middle English *eighte* from Old English *eahta:* akin to German *acht*, Latin *octo*, Greek *okto*, and Sanskrit *asta*
- One hundred lunar cycles: eight solar years (2,920 days), called a Great Year, according to Graves.[34] My reckoning puts the solar as 365.25 x 8 = 2,922, and the lunar as 99 x 29.53 = 2,923.47.
- One full Venus pentacle cycle: eight solar years.[35] (See chapter 10 and "Some Things about 13" in this chapter.)
- An eight-ray "rosette" star was the ancient symbol for Inanna, Ishtar, and the planet Venus[36] The same shape appears on maps as the Compass Rose, marking the four cardinal directions and their intermediaries.
- The Sanskrit origin of "eight" is *asta*, very similar to *aster*, the Greek work for "star."
- Eight is a common number in the substructure of inanimate things, for example, minerals.[37]
- Odin traveled on Sleipnir, an eight-leg horse.
- The lemniscate, or sideways-8, symbolizes infinity. This is sometimes shown on a globe as the *analemma*, the 8-loop of the Sun's annual (and endless) motion to-and-fro between the Tropics of Cancer and Capricorn, illustrating not only Earth's tilt but its slight wobble as well.

- In ancient tradition, the twenty-four runes of the Elder Futhark are divided into three groups of eight, and each group was called an *aett*.[38]

- The number 8 symbolized fertility in Mediterranean mythology.[39] Did this derive from the lemniscate as a symbol of eternity? Or from the analemma? Or from the figure-8 dance of the honeybee?[40]

Figure 12-11 Eight-point rosette

- That great populist scrying tool, the Magic 8 Ball. "Eight ball" comes from the game of pool, which opens with fifteen balls arranged in a "magical triangle" with five balls along each edge. *(Figure 12-13.)* Sinking the 8-ball, even accidentally, automatically ends the game. From this association with endings, finality, and fate came the phrase "behind the 8-ball" (for one who feels like the uncomfortable victim of fate) and the divinatory Magic 8 Ball.

Figure 12-12 Lemniscate

- The seven notes of the diatonic scale become a full octave when the first note is repeated—an octave higher—at the end of the sequence: C D E F G A B C. It's the same diatonic scale we met earlier, the basis for most Western music, expanded into an octave (meaning 8) with the final Do. Besides being the basis for most Western music, we can now sing the complete Do-Re-Mi-Fa-So-La-Ti-Do.

- *Synonyms and related words:* Octagon, octagonal, octave, octavo (from printing: a large sheet of paper folded down into eight leaves), octopus, October, octad, oct-, octo-, octa-

Figure 12-13 Triangle 8-ball

- Can symbolize rejuvenation, eternity, change, inspiration, evolution

Some Things about 9

- *Tarot:* Card IX, the Hermit (also, when reduced, Card XVIII, the Moon)
- The Square of the Moon is an order-9 square.
- *Word origin:* Middle English from Old English *nigon*; German *neun*, Latin *novem*, Greek *ennea*, and Sanskrit *nava*
- Any number that can be reduced to 9 is divisible by 9, for example, 108, 216, 333, 342, 873.
- 3 x 3 triples the cosmic power of 3, making 9 the number of fulfillment.
- Nine Muses: Calliope (epic poetry and eloquence), Clio (history), Erato (love poetry), Euterpe (music and lyric poetry), Melpomene (tragedy), Polyhymnia (oratory or sacred poetry), Terpsichore (dance and choral song), Thalia (comedy), and Urania (astronomy)
- Nine Giantesses turned the great Norse cosmic mill and shared the mother-hood of Heimdahl, who guarded Bifrost, the Rainbow Bridge between Earth and Asgard. In another version of Heimdahl's tale, he was born from nine waves enchanted by Odin.[41] Fittingly, the ninth rune, Hagalaz, is assigned to Heimdahl.[42]
- Nine Companions versus nine Ring-Wraiths in Tolkien's *The Lord of the Rings*
- "A cat has nine lives."
- To the Nicaraguans, the air and the nine winds were ruled by the god Chiquinau [43]

Figure 12-14 Nine dots forming a labyrinth's seed diagram

- Nine dots (*Figure 12-14*) can form the basis for an alternative labyrinth's seed diagram,[44] different from the dot-and-cross "seed" derived from the order-9 Square of the Moon.
- Nine sacred woods for a Beltane fire: Birch (representing the Goddess), oak (the God), fir (birth), willow (death), rowan (magic), apple (love), grapevine (joy), hazel (wisdom), and hawthorn (purity and the month of May)
- In *feng shui*, there are nine "cures" to correct misplaced energies.[45]
- Woden hung on Yggdrasil, the World Tree, for nine days and nine nights in self-sacrifice to earn sacred knowledge, including comprehension of the Runes.

- Among a crane's sacred associations—its dance and footprints are credited with inspiring written language—the bird was believed to take nine steps before leaping into flight.[46]
- Celtic myth describes love goddess Blodeuwedd's fingers as being "whiter than the ninth wave of the sea," and that she is created from the flowers of nine plants, including meadow-sweet, broom, and oak.[47]
- In ancient Rome, the guest lists of dinner parties were composed along numeric lines: "No fewer than the [three] Fates, nor more than the [nine] Muses."[48]
- *Synonyms and related words:* Ennead, novena (a prayer said for nine days), November, nonagon, noven-, nona-, ennea-, enne-
- Can symbolize completion, fulfillment, gestation, experience, self-awareness

Some Things about 10

- Reduces to 1: 1 + 0 = 1
- *Tarot:* Card X, the Wheel of Fortune
- *Word origin:* Middle English from Old English *tien*, German *zehn*, Latin *decem*, Greek *deka*, and Sanskrit *dasa*. These all trace back to the Indo-European *dekm*, meaning "two hands."
- Decimal: Numbered or ordered by 10s; a number containing a decimal point
- The familiar "count-down" starts at 10: Ten, nine, eight, seven . . .
- Ten was considered by the Pythagoreans to be the number of everything.
- *Synonyms and related words:* Decagon, decade, tithe (from tenth), decahedron, December, decad, decimate (divide by 10), decathalon, decapod (literally "10 feet," for example, squids and others with ten tentacles), decimal, dec-, deci-, deca-
- Can symbolize transformation, transition, results, regeneration

Some Things about 11

- Reduces to 2: 1 + 1 = 2 (*Note*: Some traditions consider 11 a "master number" that should not be reduced.)

- A prime number
- *Tarot:* Card XI, Justice (or Strength)—whichever card is used, the eleventh card is the midpoint in the numbered Major Arcana group.
- While 10 was revered, by contrast 11 was considered by some traditions to be suspect: If 10 symbolizes completeness, 11 must be too much.[49] Visions of *Spinal Tap:* The fictional supergroup's amps had volume knobs that cranked up to a logic-impaired 11.[50]
- An 11-related math trick (from an Indian text, the *Ganitasârasamgraha*, circa 850 CE)[51] is shown in *Figure 12-15.*

**Eleven and other 1-numbers,
squared (multiplied by themselves)**

$$11^2 = 121$$
$$111^2 = 12321$$
$$1111^2 = 1234321$$
$$11111^2 = 123454321$$
$$111111^2 = 12345654321$$
$$1111111^2 = 1234567654321$$
$$11111111^2 = 123456787654321$$
$$111111111^2 = 12345678987654321$$

**The sums are always
palindromes**

Figure 12-15 11-squared palindrome

Some Things about 12

- Reduces to 3: $1 + 2 = 3$
- *Tarot*: Card XII, the Hanged Man
- Twelve equals one dozen. The *Poetic Edda* makes reference to a "long hundred," which meant 120, or 12 x 10.[12][52]
- Twelve inches to one foot
- Twelve months to the year

- Twelve tribes of Israel, twelve prophets, twelve sibyls, twelve disciples (both Christ and Mithra)
- In old style British currency, one shilling was twelve pence.
- The twelve-note chromatic scale (seven diatonic notes plus their sharps or flats). From *chroma*, for the "color" the additional notes provide: C C# D D# E F F# G G# A A# B
- Twelve signs of the zodiac, twelve houses in an astrological chart
- Twelve days of Christmas, twelve labors of Hercules, twelve stars in the crown of the biblical woman clothed in the Sun (an allegorical solar eclipse, describing the narrow ring of sunlight sometimes visible around the black disk of the Moon, at which point stars become visible?)
- Can symbolize maturation, fulfillment (that is, all things in their right time)

Some Things about 13

- Reduces to 4: 1 + 3 = 4
- Both a Fibonacci series number and a prime number
- *Tarot:* Card XIII, Death
- Mythical groups of thirteen: King Arthur and his original twelve Round Table knights; Baldur and his twelve judges; Odysseus and his twelve companions; Romulus and his twelve shepherds; Roland and the twelve peers of France; Jacob and his twelve sons; Danish Hrolf and his twelve Berserkers.[53]
- Judge plus twelve -member jury
- From one Winter Solstice to the next Winter Solstice, we will truly see either thirteen Full Moons or thirteen New Moons, but not thirteen full lunar cycles. This is sort of a "moon myth" based on the idea of a 28-day Moon cycle, instead of the true 29.53 days. One value of thinking in thirteen Moons is to shake loose of standard calendar/clock time and work more imaginatively. However . . .
- Venus' year is 224.7 "Earth days" long. Earth's year is 365.25 days. Thirteen "Venus years" are darn near equal to eight Earth years: 224.7 x 13 = 2,921.1 days, 365.25 x 8 = 2,922 days.

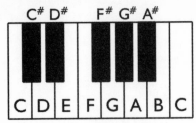

Fibonacci at the piano—2, 3, 5, 8, 13:
The 13-note chromatic octave,
made up of 8 white keys and 5 black
keys in groups of 2 and 3.

Figure 12-16 Piano keyboard in Fibonacci terms

- Thirteen treasures of Britain: Sword, basket, drinking horn, chariot, halter, knife, cauldron, whetstone, garment, pan, platter, chessboard, mantle[59]

- A "baker's dozen" is thirteen. Back when bread was price controlled and sold by weight, bakers might add a thirteenth roll as insurance against the sale coming up short.

- The eight notes of the diatonic octave plus their sharps or flats become the thirteen-note chromatic octave: C C# D D# E F F# G G# A A# B C. *(Figure 12-16.)*

- In some *bas reliefs*, neo-Hittite Mother Goddess Kubaba (who evolved into the Phrygian Cybele) is depicted with thirteen-petalled flowers on her crown.[55,56]

- The Babylonians used a base-60 number system, in which 12 is crucial. By exceeding 12, 13 is outside of that system, which may have been why the Babylonians considered the number unlucky.[57] Some believe the Christian Church fostered fear about 13 as a way of demonizing a number with many pagan associations. There's even a name for fear of 13: triskaidekaphobia.

- The Zulu culture recognizes a thirteenth zodiacal constellation, the Whale, Umkhomo, which rules between December 28 and January 6. For the Zulu, 13 is a holy number, and those born under Umkhomo are considered to be seekers, healers, and especially blessed people who do sacred work in the world.[58]

- Persian tradition: Stay out of your house on the thirteenth day after the New Year to avoid bad luck in the coming year.[59]

Some Things about 14

- Reduces to 5: 1 + 4 = 5
- *Tarot:* Card XIV, Temperance
- Each Minor Arcana Tarot suit has fourteen cards.
- Among some central Asian tribes, a "soul ladder"—a post with fourteen notches cut into it—was used to mark graves and helped the souls ascend.[60]
- In J. R. R. Tolkien's *The Hobbit*, Bilbo Baggins is invited to be the fourteenth member of a quest specifically to avoid the number 13.
- In old style British weights and measures, one "stone" equals fourteen pounds.
- A Math Fable: Osiris was murdered in the twenty-eighth year of his reign by his brother Set, who cut Osiris' body into fourteen pieces that Isis had to find and reassemble. This sounds like a moon metaphor: The Moon grows Full over fourteen nights and is then "dismembered" over fourteen nights. The Moon is hidden, then "reassembled" as it waxes. Osiris' reassembly allows Isis to become pregnant, apropos the Moon and fertility.

Some Things about 15

- Reduces to 6: 1 + 5 = 6
- *Tarot:* Card XV, The Devil
- An approximate half of the 29.53-day lunar cycle
- There are twenty-four 15-day "months" in the Hindu calendar.
- Going forth from her parents' home, Mary ascended fifteen steps into the temple where she was dedicated to service (ah, but which temple?)[61]

Some Things about 16

- Reduces to 7: 1 + 6 = 7
- *Tarot:* Card XVI, the Tower
- *Magdala* means "tower," so Mary Magdalene means Mary of the Tower.[62] In some retellings of her story, Mary Magdalene was a priestess in a goddess religion in which sacred sexuality was part of some rituals.

Some Things about 17

- Reduces to 8: $1 + 7 = 8$
- A prime number
- *Tarot:* Card XVII, the Star
- In the Elder Futhark, the seventeenth rune is Tiwaz, which Nordic star lore identified as the North Star, the point of Frigga's spindle.[63] This equates again with the idea of goddesses spinning our fate from the tangled "raw wool" of life's potentialities.[64]
- Venus' synodic period is 584 days (see Chapter 10), which reduces to 17. Venus has an 8-year cycle repeating its celestial star pattern. An eight-ray star (17 also reduces to 8) was an ancient symbol for both Inanna and Ishtar, both of whom were identified with Venus, the Morning and Evening Star.[65] Since the Tarot's Star card Number XVII often pictures its main Star as eight-pointed, perhaps Venus is the origin of the Tarot's Star.
- In Christian mysticism, 17 was associated with the star of the Magi.[66]
- We find seventeen syllables in Japanese *haiku*, arranged in three lines of five, seven, and five syllables.

Some Things about 18

- Reduces to 9: $1 + 8 = 9$
- *Tarot*: Card XVIII, the Moon
- Eighteen, the number of the Tarot's Moon, reduces to 9, the number of the planetary Square of the Moon.
- The length of a recurring eclipse cycle is eighteen-plus years. This cycle signaled eclipses at maximum lunar declinations, with especially high tides and especially bright moonlit nights. At Stonehenge, an impending lunar eclipse on the Winter Solstice would be forewarned if the Full Moon nearest the Winter Solstice rose directly over the Heel Stone.[67] Chimney Rock, a Chaco Canyon outlier site in southern Colorado, is also thought to mark this eclipse cycle, as might portions of Chaco Canyon itself. Many of Chaco Canyon's buildings are precisely aligned to solstice-Sun-at-noon points, and to rising and setting lunar declinations.[68]

- The Greek musical scale had eighteen notes, symbolic of wholeness.[69]
- In Egyptian art, the formal and very stylized human figure was drawn on a grid, 18 squares tall, sole-of-foot to brow.[69, 70]

Some Things about 19

- Reduces to 1: $1 + 9 = 10$; $1 + 0 = 1$
- A prime number
- *Tarot:* Card XIX, the Sun
- The not quite 19-year (average 18.61 years) recurring eclipse cycle mentioned in "Some Things about 18." The eclipse cycle takes between eighteen and nineteen years, and the Tarot's eighteenth and nineteenth cards represent the Moon and the Sun, the two planets necessary for those eclipses.
- See Chapter 1 on counting for the Moon's 19-year Metonic cycle.
- Practitioners of the Baha'i faith meet every nineteen days for their religious observances and track the year as nineteen months of nineteen days each, based on their numerical values of the word *wahid*, meaning "One," which is both a name of God and a unifying principle.[71]

Some Things about 20

- Reduces to 2: $2 + 0 = 2$
- *Tarot:* Card XX, Judgment
- Synonyms and related words: score, twentieth, vicenary, vicennial
- The Maya, Yoruba, and a few other cultures have vigesimal number systems, that is, based on 20.[72]
- Twenty "baby teeth"
- In British currency, one pound—1£—was twenty shillings.

Some Things about 21

- Reduces to 3: $2 + 1 = 3$
- A Fibonacci series number

- *Tarot*: Card XXI, the World
- The twenty-first Greek letter, *phi* or *Φ*, now stands for the Golden Ratio, which esoterically symbolizes the manifestation of Spirit in the world of form.[73,74]
- The great Buddhist Goddess Tara appears in twenty-one different forms.[75]
- The Tarot's twenty-two Major Arcana cards are numbered from 0 to 21, both of which are Fibonacci numbers.
- There are twenty-one possible combinations when rolling a pair of cubical dice: 1-1, 1-2, 1-3, 1-4, 1-5, 1-6; 2-2, 2-3, 2-4, 2-5, 2-6; 3-3, 3-4, 3-5, 3-6; 4-4, 4-5, 4-6; 5-5, 5-6; and 6-6. With a single die, the total spots on all six sides added together is 21: $1 + 2 + 3 + 4 + 5 + 6$.

Some Things about 22

- Reduces to 4: $2 + 2 = 4$ (*Note:* Some traditions consider 22 a "master number" that should not be reduced.)
- There are twenty-two cards in Tarot's Major Arcana, and number 22 is an alternate number for Card 0, the Fool.
- Twenty-two letters in the Hebrew alphabet, which connects with a variety of metaphysical systems including the Tarot and the Kabbalah.
- A twenty-two-year recurring sunspot-and-solar flare cycle influences Earth's weather.[76]
- Twenty-two different numbers by which a circle's 360 degrees can be evenly divided: 2, 3, 4, 5, 6, 8, 9, 10, 12, 15, 18, 20, 24, 30, 36, 40, 45, 60, 72, 90, 120, and 180.

Some Things about 23

- Reduces to 5: $2 + 3 = 5$
- A prime number
- Twenty-three pairs of human chromosomes[77]

Some Things about 28

- Reduces to 1: $2 + 8 = 10$; $1 + 0 = 1$
- A twenty-eight-year solar cycle is used for calculating the date of Easter. Math minded monk the Venerable Bede counted these years on finger-and-thumb joints of both hands to keep track.[78]
- Twenty-eight is the Pythagoreans' next "perfect" number after 6. You get to 28 by adding the first seven numbers together: $1 + 2 + 3 + 4 + 5 + 6 + 7 = 28$. Seven is a number that betokens the seven "planets," so that's all magical and dandy, but what makes it perfect is that you can divide 28 by various numbers—1, 2, 4, 7, and 14. If you add those same numbers together—$1 + 2 + 4 + 7 + 14$—you'll get 28. "Perfect" numbers are rare, so don't take them for granted. After 6 and 28, there isn't another until we get to 496.[79,80]
- There are twenty-eight letters in the Arabic alphabet.

Some Things about 40

- Reduces to 4: $4 + 0 = 4$
- The Babylonians knew that the Pleiades disappeared from view for forty-days each year, and the disappearance coincided with their rainy season.[81] The reappearance of the Pleiades was celebrated as the Babylonian New Year Festival. The importance of the number 40 shows up in other cultures as well: forty days of Lent, forty years of desert wandering by the Hebrews, forty days of isolation upon arrival in a Roman port (this practice survives in our word *quarantine*), a flooding storm that lasts for forty days.
- In Islam, memorials for the deceased are conducted forty days after death.[82]
- The annual date of the Catholic holy day Candlemas or the Purification, February 2, was forty days after Christmas, based on ancient laws that considered a woman "unclean" following childbirth. Women were barred from specific activities until they were ceremonially "purified" forty days after giving birth.[83] I like to think this was just a patriarchal explanation for the new mother staying home to rest and bond with the new baby.

Some Things about 42

- Reduces to 6: 4 + 2 = 6
- In the Egyptian Book of the Dead, the deceased must pass forty-two judges.[84]
- "Two and forty hours" is the time Shakespeare's Juliet will pass in her "seeming death."
- Forty-two symbolizes "life, the Universe and everything."[85]

Some Things about 47

- Reduces to 2: 4 + 7 = 11; 1 + 1 = 2
- A prime number
- The number of strings on a concert harp
- Fans of the television spy-drama *Alias* will recall that tech whiz Marshall liked 47, because it's a prime number. In subsequent episodes, the number 47 reappeared with a vengeance.

Some Things about 49

- Reduces to 4: 4 + 9 = 13; 1 + 3 = 4
- In the Tibetan Book of the Dead, the death-to-rebirth journey takes forty-nine days.[86]

Some Things about 50

- The fifty symbols used when writing in Sanskrit also made up the fifty skulls in the necklace of goddess Kali.[87]

Some Things about 55

- Reduces to 1: 5 + 5 = 10; 1 + 0 = 1
- A Fibonacci number: 0, 1, 1, 2, 3, 5, 8, 13, 21, 34, 55
- Respected by the Pythagoreans as the sum of the first 10 numbers: 1 + 2 + 3 + 4 + 5 + 6 + 7 + 8 + 9 + 10 = 55

Some Things about 56

- Reduces to 2: $5 + 6 = 11$; $1 + 1 = 2$
- Calculated from three 18.61-year recurrences, 56 is the smallest number capable of accurately tracking eclipse cycles over hundreds of years. This is a possible explanation for the fifty-six Aubrey Holes at Stonehenge, as first proposed by astronomer Gerald S. Hawkins in the 1960s.[88]
- There are fifty-six cards in the Tarot's Minor Arcana.

Some Things about 60

- Sixty is the smallest number that can be evenly divided by each of the first 6 numbers: 1, 2, 3, 4, 5, and 6.

Some Things about 64

- Reduces to 1: $6 + 4 = 10$; $1 + 0 = 1$
- Sixty-four cells in an order-8 magical square and on a chess- or /checkerboard
- Sixty-four hexagrams in the *I Ching*
- And of course, the Beatles song, "When I'm Sixty-Four"
- The Eye of Horus, or *oudjat*, portrays a human eye and eyebrow merged with a falcon's distinctive eye markings. *(Figure 12-17.)* Horus, son of Isis and Osiris, fought repeatedly with his uncle Set to avenge Osiris' death.

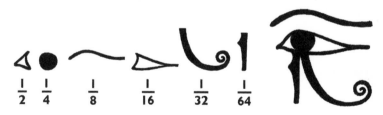

Figure 12-17 Eye of Horus

In one battle, Set tore out Horus' eye, ripped it apart, and scattered the six pieces throughout Egypt. With the help of Thoth, god of magic and wisdom, the eye was found, Horus was healed and made complete again, and the *oudjat*—eye became a symbol of wholeness and clarity. The *oudjat*—disassembled again—was used hieroglyphically to signify fractions. Separately, these six parts add up to only $^{63}/_{64}$, leaving one portion—$^{1}/_{64}$—as tribute for ibis-headed Thoth, the patron of scribes, in exchange for his blessing to any scribe who seeks and accepts his protection.[89] The shape of the *oudjat* gradually became the Rx symbol used for prescriptions, which ideally bring wholeness.[90]

CHAPTER 13

A Tale in Which Gods Do Math

Once upon a time, there was a Sky goddess named Nut and an Earth god named Geb.[1] They were siblings, children of the same parents, Air god Shu and Moisture goddess Tefnut. Nut and Geb fell in love with each other. Perhaps each was drawn by the very differentness of the other, or maybe they were intrigued by the variety and power of the interactions between them.

Their love angered their grandfather Ra, who was god of the Sun. Sky-Nut and Earth-Geb were two separate beings, and Ra intended for them to remain so. Otherwise, there'd be no room between Sky and Earth for anything else. Ra commanded Shu, the god of Air, to keep the Nut and Geb apart, and Shu tried, but he failed. Earth and Sky met and made love, and Nut conceived. Ra was furious. As Sun God—and hence a ruler of Time—he declared that he wouldn't allow Nut to give birth on any day of any month, in any month of the year.

Wise ibis-headed Thoth, Master of Numbers, Astronomy, and Measurements, took pity on Nut and Geb. Devising a plan to help them, Thoth went to play draughts with the Moon itself. Carefully playing, carefully wagering, Thoth won a $\frac{1}{72}$ portion of the Moon's light. From this $\frac{1}{72}$ portion of moonlight, Thoth created a five-day period that belonged to no month, five days outside Ra's control. On these five new days, Nut was able to bear her five divine children: Osiris, Horus, Set, Isis, and Nephthys.

The number of days in the early Egyptian year was 360, the total of twelve Moon-months of thirty days each. Thoth was initially a Moon god, another ruler of time, and his narrow and curving ibis beak is a visual echo of the Moon's own crescent. Thoth's renowned wisdom led him (and his human devotees) to understand that the Moon's monthly style of timekeeping wasn't really synchronized with the Sun's annual method.

You'll recall that when creating a star within a circle, each of a pentacle's five points is 72° from the next around the circle's 360° rim. Nothing too surprising there, since 360 divided by 5 equals 72. In this myth, that calculation is reversed: 360 (days or degrees) is divided by 72, and the result is 5. Here, this means that the $\frac{1}{72}$ portion of light that Thoth has won from the Moon represents five new days. How appropriate that Thoth accomplishes this by playing draughts! This is an ancient game similar to checkers—a checkered board with alternating squares of color, like alternating bright days and dark nights, a magical square indeed, perfect for a game in which light and time itself are being wagered. (We now associate both the 8-by-8 checkerboard grid and the intellectually clever Thoth with the planet Mercury.)

Those five days that Thoth won, besides allowing for the birth of five new deities, also confirm the vital understanding that while a circle consists of 360 degrees, a solar year has 365 days. While that's close to 360, it's certainly not identical, and the discrepancy is a crucial distinction for any culture that cares about accurate timekeeping.

This is how Thoth helped Nut and Geb.

This is how Thoth made harmony between the disparate cycles of Sun and Moon.

CHAPTER 14

Summing Up

We've looked at math and at some snippets of its mystical history, and we've looked at numbers. Now what?

Many numerology books show ways in which we can analyze our names or birth dates, reduced to a single digit, as we've done throughout the book. The final numbers are purported to give a general reading about who we are.

I first encountered this practice as a child, and remember being truly alarmed by the pat descriptions given for each 1-through-9 number. Was life really so preordained, so limited? Was I ultimately just a number? Maybe so. By adulthood, we're identified as numbers instead of names in many of our dealings with the world at large—Social Security, company ID badges, telephone extensions, charge cards, drivers' licenses, and so many more.

Really, the last place I want numbers to identify me is in the spiritual aspects of my life. So play with your personal numbers if you like—the numbers aren't the problem; it's the conclusions potentially drawn from them-but then use your numbers in creative ways that expand your sense of self rather than attempting to narrowly define it. Likewise, while there are plenty of books giving "recipes" for effective spells and rituals, often with very specific numerical instructions (how many herbs to include, how many days to do something), there are excellent reasons to deviate from these plans.

For one thing, following the spell recipes of others is a bit like expecting every recipe in every cookbook to please your personal sense of taste. If spellwork were food, we'd know to add more chilies or leave out the peanuts. We trust our taste buds and aren't afraid to say, "I hate nutmeg, so I left it out." Does the author come around to check that you obeyed their instructions? Of course not! Who's going to eat this, the author or you?

Spellwork is like learning to trust our spiritual taste buds. Begin by doing a spell as written, if you like, but don't hesitate to make adjustments to customize it. Who's going to empower this spell and then live with the results, the author or you?

Which brings us to the other, absolutely key reason to boldly adapt and personalize your spellwork: You get better results. As I wrote back in Chapter 4 on the Days of the Week, what the divine energies of the Universe respond to isn't our ability to obey some other humanoid's instructions.

What they heed is the sincere call that goes out from each individual heart. And each of us is the best judge of how to most effectively express this. Remember Chapter 0, the first in this book: You have a circle of protection, embracing, expansive, and ready to safely contain all possibilities. In magical workings, our intuition—our heart-sense of what to do—is the most valuable and profoundly powerful ingredient we have. To be truly effective as magical tools, numbers need to be used with intuitive flexibility.

So we start with our Zero, our circle of protection, our empty vessel waiting to be filled. Remember: Even before we were born, we already embodied the Golden Ratio. Now, we can lose ourselves in the dance of measuring time as tempo (a good rhythm section helps). We can remember the phi at our fingertips as we shape mudrâs to the Moon. We can watch Venus in the sky and feel the pentacle she's drawing around us. We can find that same star shape hidden within an apple, and the fruit's colors are those of the Triple Goddess: white for the Maiden's newness, red for the Mother's fertility, and black for the Crone's depth and boundlessness. And those same black seeds simultaneously contain the future.

"New Math"? This is the Old Math, and there's no "wrong" way to do it. This math is as basic as a heartbeat.

As easy as 1, 2, 3. . . .

Notes

Chapter 1: Counting

1 Pollack, *Body of the Goddess,* p. 67.
2 Ifrah, *Numbers,* p. 480.
3 Joseph, *Crest,* pp. 306 and 312.
4 Ifrah, *Numbers,* p. 364.
5 Ibid., p. 365.
6 Kaplan, *The Nothing That Is,* p. 49.
7 Ibid., p. 66.
8 Swetz, *Legacy of the Luoshu,* p. 80.
9 Joseph, *The Crest of the Peacock,* p. 320. Joseph mentions the "casting out nines" trick by name, but gives a different example of it.
10 Keller and Keller, *Complete Book of Numerology,* p. 12.
11 Ifrah, *Numbers,* p. 50.
12 Ibid., pp. 49–50.
13 *American Heritage Dictionary,* "Metonic."
14 *American Ephemeris,* 1991–2000 and 2001–2010.
15 Pennick, *Games,* pp. 32–36.
16 Ibid.

Chapter 2: The Moon

1 Rush, *Moon, Moon,* pp. 300–335.
2 Hawkins, *Stonehenge Decoded,* p. 152.

3 Pickover, *Passion*, p. 267.

4 Mead, *Thrice Greatest Hermes,* Bk. I, p. 38.

5 Ibid, p. 45.

6 Ibid, p. 51.

7 Ibid, p. 223.

8 Ibid, p. 83.

9 Ibid, p. 40.

10 Ibid, p. 82.

11 Mead, *Thrice Greatest Hermes,* Bk. II, pp. 155–56.

Chapter 3: Measurements:

1 Brunés, *Secrets of Ancient Geometry,* vol I, pp. 46–47.

2 Ibid, p. 44.

3 Gillings, *Mathematics*, p. 220.

Chapter 4: The Days of the Week

1 I'm told the ancient Sumerians were well aware of the outer
   planets. For example, Uranus can be visible to the naked eye,
   but is so faint and moves so very slowly that it's nearly
   indistinguish able from the stars beyond it. In any case,
   information about additional planets wasn't "discovered" in
   Europe until much later.

2 Hakim, *Story of Science,* p. 30.

3 Monaghan, *O Mother Sun,* pp. 49–60.

4 Ibid., p. 61.

5 Pollack, *Body of the Goddess,* pp. 20–21.

6 Monaghan, *New Book of Goddesses and Heroines,* p. 284.

7 Monaghan, *O Mother Sun,* p. 114.

8 Monaghan, *New Book of Goddesses and Heroines,* this and
   subsequent goddess information.

9 Forty, *Classic Mythology,* this and other deity information.

10 Farrar and Farrar, *Witches' God,* this and other god information.

11 Pennick, *Games,* p. 100, and Graves, *White Goddess,* p. 259.

12 Lawrence, *Numerology,* p. 151. The entries on musical notes are taken by Lawrence from Pythagoras.

13 "The Mystery of Chaco Canyon," Anna Sofaer and the Solstice Project, PBS program.

14 Farrar and Farrar, *Witches' God,* pp. 26, 200, and 202.

15 Forty, *Classic Mythology,* p. 107.

16 For insight into Mars and commercial kitchens, many thanks to Marilyn Megenity of Denver's Mercury Café.

17 Stewart, *Hollow Hills,* pp. 220–23.

18 The term "non-ordinary reality," widely used among shamanic practitioners, is usually credited to Carlos Castaneda.

19 Graves, *Greek Myths,* Vol. I, p. 51.

20 Walker, *Women's Encyclopedia,* p. 392.

21 Wolkstein and Kramer, *Inanna,* pp. 39 and 47.

22 Graves, *Greek Myths,* Vol. I, pp. 27, 38, and 41.

Chapter 5: The Magical Squares

1 Joseph, *The Crest of the Peacock,* pp. 149–51.

2 Pickover, *Zen,* pp. 8–10.

3 Joseph, *The Crest of the Peacock,* p. 151.

4 Hale, *Encyclopedia of Feng Shui,* p. 24.

5 A friend and I checked our respective assortment of books containing magical squares to see if each planet's layout varied from book to book. None did, but we both found errors aplenty. These came in three flavors: a number used more than once per square, a sequential number omitted, and numbers that were just plain wrong (for example, a sixteen-cell square with 17). Whether these were typos, or the apocryphal "information too powerful and secret to be transmitted correctly," who knows?

After that, I rechecked the squares in this book for accuracy. Please use care in creating yours, too.

6 Pickover, *Zen,* p. 11.

7 Schimmel, *Mystery of Numbers,* p. 215.

8 Conway, *Magic,* p. 189.

9 Swetz, *Legacy of the Luoshu,* pp. 83–84.

10 Pickover, *Zen,* pp. 12–13.

11 Brands, *First American,* pp. 206–7.

12 Pickover, *Zen,* pp. 19–22.

13 Swetz, *Legacy of the Luoshu,* p. 26.

14 Bosman, *Meaning and Philosophy of Numbers,* p. 18.

15 Pennick, *Magical Alphabets,* pp. 13–21.

16 Ibid., p. 53.

17 Guthrie, *Pythagorean Sourcebook,* p. 53.

18 Pickover, *Zen,* pp. 81–82.

19 Workshop with George Moyer, at DragonFest 2000.

20 *Concise Columbia Encyclopedia,* "moon."

21 Upgren, *Turtle and the Stars,* pp. 113–14, 167.

22 Hawkins, *Beyond Stonehenge,* pp. 184–85.

Chapter 6: The Knight's Tour and Templar Codes?

1 Pickover, *Zen,* pp. 210–11.

2 Begg, *Black Virgin,* p. 16.

3 Lunn, *Da Vinci Code Decoded,* p. 53.

4 Begg, *Black Virgin,* p. 109.

5 Starbird, *Woman with the Alabaster Jar,* p. 76.

6 Hopkins, Simmans, and Wallace-Murphy, *Rex Deus,* pp. 18–19.

7 Lunn, *Da Vinci Code Decoded,* p. 28.

8 Charpentier, *Mysteries of Chartres Cathedral,* pp. 30–32.

9 Pearson, *France 2005—Let's Go,* p. 302.

10 Hopkins, Simmans, and Wallace-Murphy, *Rex Deus,* pp. 153–55.

11 Begg, *Black Virgin,* p. 130.

12 Starbird, *Woman with the Alabaster Jar,* p. 75.

13 Begg, *Black Virgin,* p. 107.

14 Lunn, *Da Vinci Code Decoded,* pp. 29–30.

15 Fanthorpe and Fanthorpe, *Templar Treasure and the Holy Grail,* pp. 78–79.

16 American Home Treasures, *DaVinci Code,* DVD.

17 Starbird, *Woman with the Alabaster Jar,* p. 62.

18 Ibid., p. 52.

19 Ibid., pp. 92–96.

20 American Home Treasures, *DaVinci Code, DVD.*

Chapter 7: Shapes and Numbers Meditation

1 Pollack, *Illustrated Guide to the Tarot,* p. 30.

2 King, *Modern Numerology,* p. 98.

3 Ibid., pp. 98–118; Zetter, *Simple Kabbalah,* pp. 135–41; Pike, *Morals and Dogma,* p. 770.

4 Thomson, *Pictures from the Heart,* p. 361.

Chapter 8: Pythagoras

1 Graves, *White Goddess,* p. 149.

2 King, *Modern Numerology,* pp. 15–16.

3 Graves, *White Goddess,* p. 281.

4 King, *Modern Numerology,* pp. 15–16.

5 Graves, *White Goddess,* p. 189n.; also Heath, *Manual of Greek Mathematics.*

Chapter 9: Fibonacci and the Golden Ratio

1 Joseph, *The Crest of the Peacock,* p. 315.

2 Doczi, *The Power of Limits,* p. 5.

3 Livio, *The Golden Ratio,* p. 5.

4   Lawlor, *Sacred Geometry*, pp. 56–8.

5   Schneider, *Beginner's Guide*, p. 154.

6   Lawlor, *Sacred Geometry*, pp. 56–58.

7   Lawlor, *Sacred Geometry*; also Doczi, *The Power of Limits*.

8   Livio, *The Golden Ratio*, p. 7.

9   Pickover, *Passion*, p. 270.

10 Livio, *The Golden Ratio*, pp. 142, 153.

Chapter 10: Venus' Pentacle

1   Hawkins, *Mindsteps,* pp. 46–69.

2   Knight and Lomas, *Uriel's Machine,* 102–3.

3   Lincoln, *Key to the Sacred Pattern,* pp. 144–45.

4   Budge, *Gods of the Egyptians,* Vol. II, p. 314.

5   Maor, *June 8, 2004—Venus in Transit,* p. 173.

Chapter 11: The Geometric Solids

1   Lippard, *Overlay,* pp. 82–83.

2   Lawlor, *Sacred Geometry,* p. 96.

3   Pickover, *Passion,* p. 356.

Chapter 12: Individual Numbers

1   *American Heritage Dictionary,* "zero." Word origin information
    on the other numbers also from here unless noted otherwise.

2   Ifrah, *Numbers,* pp. 361–2.

3   Redmond, *Drummers,* p. 181, for this and all following drum-
    sound information.

4   Motz and Weaver, *Story of Mathematics,* p. 25.

5   Begg, *Black Virgin,* p. 43.

6   Lawlor, *Sacred Geometry,* p. 75.

7   Menninger, *Number Words and Number Symbols,* p. 174.

8   Hopper, *Medieval Number Symbolism,* p. 5.

9   Begg, *Black Virgin,* pp. 220–21; and Graves, *White Goddess,* p. 191.

10 Walker, *Women's Encyclopedia,* p. 351.

11 Ibid., p. 51.

12 Hopper, *Medieval Number Symbolism,* pp. 4–5.

13 Walker, *Women's Encyclopedia,* p. 730.

14 Hawkins, *Mindsteps,* p. 41.

15 Begg, *Black Virgin,* p. 82.

16 Hendrix, from the album *Are You Experienced?*

17 Knight and Lomas, *Uriel's Machine,* pp.102–3.

18 Graves, *White Goddess,* p. 201.

19 Redmond, *Drummers,* p. 34.

20 Tresidder, *Symbols and Their Meanings,* p. 167.

21 Walker, *Women's Encyclopedia,* p. 523.

22 Lawlor, *Sacred Geometry,* p. 58.

23 Keller and Keller, *Complete Book of Numerology,* p. 15.

24 Larrington, *Poetic Edda,* p. 57.

25 Monaghan, *New Book of Goddesses and Heroines,* p. 124.

26 Hauck, *Emerald Tablet,* p. 314.

27 Graves, *White Goddess,* p. 208.

28 Kinstler, *Moon Under Her Feet.*

29 Walker, *Women's Encyclopedia,* pp. 452, 885–86.

30 Schneider, *Beginner's Guide,* p. 221.

31 Apostolos-Cappadona, *Women in Religious Art,* p. 74.

32 Swetz, *Legacy of the Luoshu,* pp. 79–80.

33 Redmond, *Drummers,* p. 75.

34 Graves, *Greek Myths,* Vol. 1, p. 141.

35 Hawkins, *Mindsteps,* pp. 46–49.

36 Apostolos-Cappadona, *Women in Religious Art,* p. 348.

37 Lawlor, *Sacred Geometry,* p. 58.

38 Pennick, *Illustrated Guide to Runes,* pp. 122–3.

39 Graves, *Greek Myths,* Vol. 1, p. 274.

40 Buxton, *Shamanic Way of the Bee*, pp. 72–75.

41 Graves, *White Goddess,* pp. 178 and 314.

42 Pennick, *Illustrated Guide to Runes,* p. 123.

43 Farrar and Farrar, *Witches' God,* p. 167.

44 Pennick, *Games,* p. 170.

45 Carter, *Move Your Stuff,* pp. 24–31.

46 Graves, *White Goddess,* p. 233.

47 Ibid., p. 314.

48 Roberts, *SPQR II,* p. 58.

49 Schimmel, *Mystery of Numbers,* p. 189.

50 *This Is Spinal Tap,* director Rob Reiner.

51 Ifrah, *Numbers,* p. 399.

52 Larrington, *Poetic Edda,* p. 270.

53 Graves, *White Goddess,* p. 201.

54 Walker, *Women's Encyclopedia,* p. 648.

55 Storm, *Egyptian Mythology,* pp. 44–45.

56 Farrar and Farrar, *Witches' Goddess,* p. 238.

57 Swetz, *Legacy of the Luoshu,* p. 79.

58 McDonald, *Mythology of the Zodiac,* pp. 21 and 85.

59 *National Geographic,* July 1999, p. 1.

60 Walker, *Women's Encyclopedia,* p. 524.

61 Apostolos-Cappadona, *Women in Religious Art,* p. 133; and Kinstler, *Moon Under Her Feet.*

62 Begg, *Black Virgin,* pp. 97, 127.

63 Gitlin-Emmer, *Lady of the Northern Lights,* pp. 78–81.

64 Pennick, *Games,* p. 30.

65 Redmond, *Drummers,* p. 78.

66 Pickover, *Zen,* p. 11.

67 Hawkins, *Mindsteps,* p. 81.

68 "The Mystery of Chaco Canyon," Anna Sofaer and the Solstice Project, PBS program.

69 Brunés, *Secrets,* Vol. 2, pp. 93 ff.

70 Lawlor, *Sacred Geometry,* p. 94.

71 Schimmel, *Mystery of Numbers,* p. 224.

72 Joseph, *Crest of the Peacock,* p. 43.

73 Lawlor, *Sacred Geometry,* p. 44.

74 Pennick, *Magical Alphabets,* p. 56.

75 Apostolos-Cappadona, *Women in Religious Art,* p. 354.

76 Prosser, "Sunspot Cycles May Be Linked,"*Denver Post,* May 4, 2003, p. 1E.

77 Shlain, *Sex, Time and Power,* p. 24.

78 Ifrah, *Numbers,* pp. 49–50.

79 Swerz, *Legacy of the Luoshu,* p. 94.

80 Livio, *Golden Ratio,* p. 33.

81 Hopper, *Medieval Number Symbolism,* p. 15.

82 Schimmel, *Mystery of Numbers,* p. 248.

83 Walker, *Women's Encyclopedia,* pp. 134–35.

84 Pennick, *Magical Alphabets,* p. 31.

85 Adams, *Hitchhiker's Guide to the Galaxy,* pp. 179–180.

86 Eliade, *Shamanism,* p. 208n.

87 Graves, *White Goddess,* p. 235.

88 Hawkins, *Mindsteps,* pp. 81ff.; and *Stonehenge Decoded,* pp. 138–40.

89 Ifrah, *Numbers,* pp. 169–70.

90 Brier, *Ancient Egyptian Magic,* p. 145.

Chapter 13: A Tale in Which Gods Do Math

1 Adapted from Farrar and Farrar, *The Witches' God.*

Bibliography

*An asterisk indicates books of particular mathematical interest.

Adams, Douglas. *The Hitchhiker's Guide to the Galaxy.* New York: Ballantine Books, 1980.

The American Ephemeris. San Diego, CA: ACS Publications, 1980.

The American Heritage Dictionary, Boston: Houghton Mifflin Co., 1989.

American Home Treasures. *The DaVinci Code: Where It All Began.* DVD, 2005.

American Masters: Robert Rauschenberg, Inventive Genius. Educational Broadcasting Corporation and Film Odyssey, Inc., 1999.

Apostolos-Cappadona, Diane. *Dictionary of Women in Religious Art.* New York: Oxford University Press, 1998.

Aveni, Anthony F. *Skywatchers of Ancient Mexico.* Austin, TX: University of Texas Press, 1980.

Begg, Ean. *The Cult of the Black Virgin.* New York: Penguin Putnam/Arkana, 1985.

Bosman, Leonard. *The Meaning and Philosophy of Numbers.* Berwick, ME: Ibis, 2005.

Brands, H. W. *The First American: The Life and Times of Benjamin Franklin.* New York: Doubleday, 2000.

Brier, Bob. *Ancient Egyptian Magic.* New York: Quill/William Morrow and Co., 1980.

*Brunés, Tons. *The Secrets of Ancient Geometry and Its Use*, Vols. I and II. Copenhagen, Denmark: Rhodos, 1967.

Budge, E. A. Wallis. *Gods of the Egyptians*, vol. II. New York: Dover Publications, 1969.

Butler, Rev. Alban. *Lives of the Saints*. New York: Benziger Brothers, 1955.

Buxton, Simon. *The Shamanic Way of the Bee*. Rochester, VT: Destiny Books, 2004.

Carter, Karen Rauch. *Move Your Stuff, Change Your Life*. New York: Fireside/Simon and Schuster, 2000.

Charpentier, Louis. *The Mysteries of Chartres Cathedral*. New York: Avon, 1975.

The Concise Columbia Encyclopedia, New York: Avon, 1983.

Conner, Randy P., David Hatfield Sparks, and Marija Sparks. *Cassells' Encyclopedia of Queer Myth, Symbol and Spirit*. London: Cassell, 1997.

Conway, David. *Magic: An Occult Primer.* New York: Bantam Books, 1972.

*Doczi, György. *The Power of Limits: Proportional Harmonies in Nature Art, and Architecture*. Boston: Shambala, 1981.

Eliade, Mircea. *Shamanism*. Princeton, NJ: Princeton University Press, 1972.

Escher, M. C. *The Graphic Work of M. C. Escher*. New York: Ballantine Books, 1971.

Fanthorpe, Lionel, and Patricia Fanthorpe. *Mysteries of Templar Treasure and the Holy Grail*. Boston: Weiser, 1992.

Farrar, Janet, and Stewart Farrar. *The Witches' God*. Custer, WA: Phoenix, 1989
———. *The Witches' Goddess*. Custer, WA: Phoenix, 1987.

Forty, Jo (ed.). *Classic Mythology*. San Diego, CA: Thunder Bay Press, 1999.

Gillings, Richard J. *Mathematics in the Time of the Pharaohs*. New York: Dover Publications, 1972.

Gitlin-Emmer, Susan. *Lady of the Northern Lights: A Feminist Guide to the Runes*. Freedom, CA: Crossing Press, 1993.

Goldsworthy, Andy. *A Collaboration with Nature*. New York: Harry N. Abrams, Inc., 1990, and other collections; and the film *Rivers and Tides: Andy Goldsworthy Working with Time*, 2001.

Graves, Robert. *The Greek Myths*. Vols. I and II. Baltimore, MD: Penguin Books, 1955, and other editions.
———. *The White Goddess*. New York: Farrar, Strauss and Giroux, 1948.

Greer, Mary K. *Tarot for Your Self*. North Hollywood, CA: Newcastle, 1984.

Guthrie, Kenneth Sylvan. *The Pythagorean Sourcebook and Library*. Grand Rapids, MI: Phanes, 1988.

Hakim, Joy. *The Story of Science: Aristotle Leads the Way*. Washington, DC: Smithsonian Books, 2004.

Hauck, Dennis William. *The Emerald Tablet*. New York: Penguin, 1999.

Hale, Gill. *The Practical Encyclopedia of Feng Shui*. London: Anness Publishing, 1999.

Hawkins, Gerald S. *Stonehenge Decoded*. New York: Dell Publishing, 1965.
———. *Beyond Stonehenge*. New York: Harper and Row, 1973.
———. *Mindsteps to the Cosmos*. New York: Harper and Row, 1983.

Heath, Sir Thomas L. *A Manual of Greek Mathematics*. New York: Dover Publications, 1963.

Jimi Hendrix, song title from the *Are You Experienced* album, 1967.

Hopkins, Marilyn, Graham Simmans, and Tim Wallace-Murphy. *Rex Deus: The True Mystery of Rennes-le-Château and the Dynasty of Jesus*. Boston: Element Books. 2000.

Hopper, Vincent Foster. *Medieval Number Symbolism: Its Sources, Meaning and Influence on Thought and Expression.* New York: Cooper Square Publishers, Inc., 1969.

*Ifrah, Georges. *The Universal History of Numbers.* New York: John Wiley and Sons, Inc., 1998.

*Joseph, George Gheverghese. *The Crest of the Peacock: Non-European Roots of Mathematics.* Princeton, NJ: Princeton University Press, 2000.

*Kaplan, Robert. *The Nothing That Is: A Natural History of Zero.* New York: Oxford University Press, 1999.

Keller, Joyce and Jack Keller. *The Complete Book of Numerology.* New York: St. Martin's Griffin, 2001.

King, John. *Modern Numerology.* London: Cassell, 1996.

Kinstler, Clysta. *The Moon Under Her Feet.* San Francisco: Harper Collins, 1991.

Knight, Christopher and Robert Lomas. *Uriel's Machine.* Gloucester, MA: Fair Winds Press, 2001.

Larrington, Carolyn. *The Poetic Edda.* New York: Oxford University Press, 1996.

*Lawlor, Robert. *Sacred Geometry: Philosophy and Practice.* New York: Thames and Hudson, 1982.

Lawrence, Shirley Blackwell. *The Secret Science of Numerology.* Franklin Lakes, NJ: New Page, 2001.

Lincoln, Henry. *Key to the Sacred Pattern.* New York: St. Martin's, 1998.

Lippard, Lucy R. *Overlay.* New York: Pantheon Books, 1983.

*Livio, Mario. *The Golden Ratio: The Story of Phi, the World's Most Astonishing Number.* New York: Broadway Books, 2002.

Lunn, Martin. *Da Vinci Code Decoded.* New York: Disinformation Co., 2004.

Maor, Eli. *June 8, 2004: Venus in Transit*. Princeton, NJ: Princeton University Press, 2000.

McDonald, Marianne. *Mythology of the Zodiac: Tales of the Constellations*. New York: Metro Books, 2000.

Mead, G. R. S. *Thrice Greatest Hermes*. Boston: Weiser, 1972.

Menninger, Karl. *Number Words and Number Symbols*. New York: Dover Publications, 1992.

Monaghan, Patricia. *The New Book of Goddesses and Heroines*. Minneapolis, MN: Llewellyn, 1997.

———. *O Mother Sun: A New View of the Cosmic Feminine*. Freedom, CA: Crossing Press, 1994.

Motz, Lloyd, and Jefferson Hane Weaver. *The Story of Mathematics*. New York: Avon Books, 1993.

The Mystery of Chaco Canyon, directed by Anna Sofaer, Bullfrog Films, 1999.

The Old Farmer's Almanac, Dublin, NH: Yankee Publishing, printed annually.

National Geographic, Vol. 196, No. 1, Tampa, FL: National Geographic Society, July 1999.

Pearson, Erin (ed.). *France 2005—Let's Go*. New York: St. Martin's Press, 2005.

Pennick, Nigel. *The Complete Illustrated Guide to the Runes*. Boston: Element Books, 1999.

*———. *Magical Alphabets*. York Beach, ME: Weiser, 1992.

———. *Secret Games of the Gods: Ancient Ritual Systems in Board Games*. York Beach, ME: Weiser, 1997.

*Pickover, Clifford A. *A Passion for Mathematics*. Hoboken, NJ: John Wiley and Sons, Inc., 2005.

———. *The Zen of Magic Squares, Circles, and Stars*. Princeton, NJ: Princeton University Press, 2002.

Pike, Albert. *Morals and Dogma of the Ancient and Accepted Scottish Rite of Freemasonry*. Richmond, VA: L. H. Jenkins, Inc., 1871.

Pollack, Rachel. *The Body of the Goddess.* Rockport, MA: Element Books, 1997.

———. *Complete Illustrated Guide to the Tarot.* New York: Gramercy Books, 1999.

Prosser, John. "Sunspot Cycles May Be Linked," *Denver Post,* May 4, 2003.

Redmond, Layne. *When the Drummers Were Women.* New York: Three Rivers Press, 1997.

Riva, Anna. *Secrets of Magical Seals.* Los Angeles, CA: International Imports, 1990.

River, Lindsay, and Sally Gillespie. *The Knot of Time.* New York: Harper and Row, 1987.

Roberts, John Maddox. *SPQR II: The Catiline Conspiracy.* New York: St. Martin's Minotaur, 2001.

Rush, Anne Kent. *Moon, Moon.* New York: Random House; and Berkeley, CA: Moon Books, 1976.

Schimmel, Annemarie. *The Mystery of Numbers.* New York: Oxford University Press, 1993.

*Schneider, Michael S. *A Beginner's Guide to Constructing the Universe.* New York: Harper Perennial, 1995.

Shlain, Leonard. *Sex, Time and Power: The Evolution of Human Mating.* New York: Viking, 2003.

Starbird, Margaret. *The Woman with the Alabaster Jar.* Santa Fe, NM: Bear & Co. 1993.

Starhawk. *The Spiral Dance.* San Francisco: Harper and Row, 1979, and other editions.

Stewart, Mary. *The Hollow Hills.* New York: William Morrow, 1973.

Storm, Rachel. *Egyptian Mythology.* New York: Lorenz Books, 2000.

Streep, Peg. *Sanctuaries of the Goddess.* Boston: Little, Brown & Co, 1994.

Swetz, Frank J. *The Legacy of the Luoshu*. Chicago: Open Court, 2002.

Teish, Luisah. *Jambalaya*. San Francisco: Harper and Row, 1985.

This Is Spinal Tap. Directed by Rob Reiner, 1984.

Thomson, Sandra A. *Pictures from the Heart*. New York: St. Martin's Griffin, 2003.

Tresidder, Jack. *Symbols and Their Meanings*. London: Friedman/Fairfax Publications, 2000.

Upgren, Arthur. *The Turtle and the Stars*. New York: Henry Holt and Co., 2002.

Walker, Barbara G. *Women's Encyclopedia of Myths and Secrets*. San Francisco: Harper and Row, 1983.

Wolkstein, Diane, and Samual Noah Kramer. *Inanna, Queen of Heaven and Earth*. New York: Harper and Row, 1983.

Zetter, Kim. *Simple Kabbalah*. Berkeley, CA: Conari Press, 1999.

Zimmerman, J. E.*Dictionary of Classical Mythology*. New York: Harper and Row, 1964.

Index

About the Author

Renna Shesso brings a life-long study of mystical traditions to her writing. Inspired by her herbalist/astrologer grandmother, her interests include into art, literature, and a long career as an art critic for *Westword, Denver's* paper in the *New Times* chain. She holds a BA in Studio Art from Colorado Women's College, and studies extensively in mythology and history, archeology, Tarot, and the vast lore of the Goddess traditions. A long time resident of Colorado, she is a shamanic practitioner, a labyrinth creator, and a teacher and priestess of Wicca.

Photo © 2005 Cynthia McKeever

To Our Readers

Weiser Books, an imprint of Red Wheel/Weiser, publishes books across the entire spectrum of occult and esoteric subjects. Our mission is to publish quality books that will make a difference in people's lives without advocating any one particular path or field of study. We value the integrity, originality, and depth of knowledge of our authors.

Our readers are our most important resource, and we value your input, suggestions, and ideas about what you would like to see published. Please feel free to contact us, to request our latest book catalog, or to be added to our mailing list.

Red Wheel/Weiser, LLC
500 Third Street, Suite 230
San Francisco, CA 94107
www.redwheelweiser.com